GOD'S TENT

The Tabernacle for Today

ALDWORTH COWAN

Fleming H. Revell Company
Old Tappan, New Jersey

Unless otherwise stated, quotations are from The Holy Bible, New International Version used by permission of Hodder and Stoughton.

The following abbreviations are used to refer to different Bible quotations:

KJV	Authorized King James Version
RSV	Revised Standard Version
NASB	New American Standard Bible
NEB	New English Bible
GNB	Good News Bible

ISBN 8007-1269-2

Published in Great Britain by Pickering & Inglis Ltd.
Copyright © 1980 by Aldworth Cowan
Published by Fleming H. Revell Company
All rights reserved
Printed in the United States of America

To Renée,
who pitched God's Tent
in our home

Contents

1 | THE EXODUS

The tenth plague had struck in Egypt, and it had struck home. All the other plagues put together had failed to achieve the release from slavery for which the children of Israel longed, but this one touched every Egyptian family and left the eldest son dead at midnight.

In the dark hours Pharaoh was called by his servants to the bedside of his eldest son only to find, lying on the bed, the lifeless body of his heir. As bewildered he paced up and down in the palace, loud cries of weeping came from the homes of his counsellors and servants as the whole populace bewailed the inexplicable death of the eldest son in every house. Then as the people ran out into the fields or entered their cattle stalls they found the same thing had happened there. The first to be born was now dead.

It was still dark when Pharaoh called for Moses and his elder brother Aaron. 'Up!' he said, 'Leave my people, you and the Israelites! Go, worship the Lord as you have requested. Take your flocks and herds ... and go.' (12:31)

During that night God's people had been observing his passover ceremony with its slain lamb and shed blood

Exodus is referred to where only the chapter and verse are given.

protecting the home from tragedy. God had said, 'This is how you are to eat it: with your cloak tucked into your belt, your sandals on your feet and your staff in your hand. Eat it in haste.' (12:11) So when Pharaoh said 'Go' they were ready to leave.

The Egyptian people willingly hastened their departure. They plied them with clothing and articles of silver and gold, little knowing that within the year, these precious metals would be used in a sacred building to worship and glorify the God the Egyptians had disdained.

Their escape route was marked out by a pillar, or column, of cloud that guided them as it moved forward during the day. By night it had the appearance of fire, so giving them not only direction but light on their journey.

Some five days later after travelling about 100 km (60 miles) the Israelites reached a critical stage of the journey. They had arrived at Yam Suph, the Sea of Reeds, and this large body of water barred their progress. To make matters worse, the news that reached them from the way they had come turned their early joy at the prospect of freedom into dismay. Pharaoh had changed his mind and sent his elite chariot corps in pursuit, to bring them back into bondage.

But in his saving power God carried out three miracles. First of all he moved the cloud behind his people so that it settled down on the approaching Egyptians, surrounding them with misty darkness and blotting out visibility. On the other side the illuminative properties of the pillar lit up the scene for the Israelites as they prepared to advance.

The second miracle was the springing up of a strong east wind which parted the waters. It dried up the soil sufficiently for the Israelites to move their wagons and flocks and cross over on a broad front while the waters were held back like a wall on either side.

The third miracle took place when morning dawned and the Egyptian charioteers followed in hot pursuit. While they crossed, the waters of the sea closed in on them. From the opposite bank the Israelites watched as the chariot wheels became clogged and, with no possible way of escape, neither man nor animal had any hope of staying alive. Soon the

bodies of Pharaoh's finest fighting unit and countless regular troops were being washed up on the shores of the sea.

This experience was important to the Israelites' understanding of the power of God. For years they had lived in a land where power was ascribed to countless false gods and in time they had become spiritually disheartened in worshipping the God of their fathers. Since the plagues which Moses had been involved in had mostly taken place in the Egyptian areas of the country, these people had not seen, or appreciated fully, God's hand at work. But now, at the beginning of their long march through the wilderness, they received dramatic and visible evidence of the saving power of the God of their fathers. This was the one who had so recently disclosed himself to Moses as Yahweh,* the personal God, the self-existent God, the actively present, saving God.

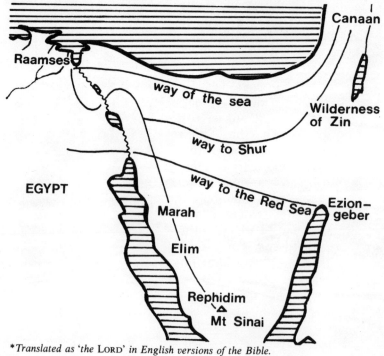

*Translated as 'the LORD' in English versions of the Bible.

4

Once the crossing of the Red Sea had been successfully made there was a choice of three roads leading to the Promised Land. The most direct route, later known as the 'Via Maris—the way of the sea' ran along the Mediterranean coast, and had the children of Israel travelled that way, they could have completed their journey in less than a month. But the Philistines were active on that route and God led them away from it knowing that if they encountered direct opposition at that stage, the Israelites would have become wearied and turned back to Egypt in defeat.

The second route was known as 'the way to Shur'. It was the same path Hagar had travelled on her attempted escape into Egypt. The third possible route known as the 'Pilgrim's Way', ran from the head of the Gulf of Suez across to the Gulf of Aquaba.

But it wasn't God's purpose to lead his people by any of these well-travelled roads. Instead, he directed them along the Gulf of Suez for a distance of more than 160 km (100 miles) and then turned them inland towards the modern Jebel Musa which is generally regarded as the Mount Sinai of the Bible.

When the Israelites left Egypt, they did not have a cohesive national identity. Years of slavery had demoralised them and they went out as a motley group of families with a tribal loyalty. They had little confidence in themselves and scarcely any in the God of their fathers. So unnerved were they that they had earlier condemned Moses' efforts to free them and urged him not to interfere.

It was therefore God's plan that the people of Israel who had no national structure, no body of laws, no army, no integrated loyalty and no authoritative pattern of approach to him, should spend a period of about one year learning these things and being built into a nation for the first time in their history.

After watching the defeat of the Egyptian army, the Israelites spent time in praise to God, then followed the cloud as it guided them southwards.

For three days they travelled and found no water on their

journey. When they did reach the small oasis of Marah the water was undrinkable, as is still the case in the modern Hawarah with which it is identified. Grumbling broke out against Moses but God instructed him to cast a particular tree into the water basin and the water became sweet and drinkable. This met their immediate need, because when they resumed their journey they found that only some 10 km (6 miles) further on there lay the delightful oasis of Elim with twelve springs of water, surrounded by seventy palm trees. It was a restful spot and for a time they camped by the water and enjoyed its refreshment and the shade provided by the trees.

Moving on again, the columns of people reached an area known as the 'wilderness of Sin' which lay between Elim and Sinai (16:1). They arrived at this plain on the fifteenth day of the second month, exactly one month after leaving captivity in Raamses.

At this point the food supplies they had brought from Egypt ran out and again considerable discontent arose against Moses and Aaron. Humanly speaking the people had real cause for alarm since the desolate area could not provide them with supplies. But they should have realised that the God who had delivered them with mighty power and miracles would never abandon them to starvation. To their leaders who had worked so hard to release them from slavery the people actually said, 'If only we had died by the LORD's hand in Egypt!' (16:3)

Moses had been attacked by the people in Egypt for attempting to release them from bondage and now within a month he was under attack once more for having succeeded in doing so. As so often happens when men and women look back on their past life, they idealised the conditions in Egypt. They chose to overlook the dreadful circumstances in which they had lived and, to his astonishment, told Moses that living there, 'we sat round pots of meat and ate all the food we wanted'.

Moses had only one place to go, or better, one Person he could turn to. He took his burden to God. As a result Aaron gathered the whole congregation together and when they stood waiting they looked towards the wilderness and saw the pillar of cloud illuminated with a glory that came from God.

God gave Moses his message. 'I have heard the grumbling of the Israelites' (16:11), he said. The people had vented their anger on Moses and Aaron but it had reached the ear of God who knows and cares when his leaders are unjustly criticised. He responded with the promise of two different kinds of food. 'At twilight you will eat meat, and in the morning you will be filled with bread. Then you will know that I am the LORD your God' (16:12).

To the Israelites it seemed a promise utterly incapable of fulfilment. A barren desert around them and yet a divine pledge that this night they would have plenty of meat! Then in the evening, the promise came true when flocks of quail covered the camp.

Quails are small, brownish, bullet-headed birds about 20 cm long. They fly low and normally roost in bushes or on the ground at night. They are swift in flight taking every advantage of the wind. But should it change course or the birds become exhausted on a long flight, the immense flock is likely to fall to the ground. It was, in fact, during the season when quail migrate en masse from the south that this incident took place.

God's second, and continuing provision, came in the form of a food that the people called manna from the Hebrew word 'man' meaning 'what?' When they saw it they asked, 'What is it?' and from that question it got its name 'manna'. It was in fact a nickname meaning a 'whatness' or, colloquially, a 'whatdyacallit'.

In appearance manna was small, round and white. It had to be gathered in the morning because it melted in the sun and ordinarily would not keep overnight. Manna had the taste of 'a wafer made with honey' (16:31) or 'butter-cakes' (Num. 11:8 NEB). It could also be baked or boiled though it was usually ground before baking. Moses described it as 'the bread the LORD has given you to eat' (16:15).

Since it did not normally keep overnight, each day the

people were to gather sufficient manna for their needs. However, on the sixth day they had to collect twice as much because God commanded that the following day would be one of rest, and no manna would fall. However, true to form, there were those in Israel who did not obey and went out on the seventh day in search of bread. They found none, and this caused God to ask a question which is still very appropriate to many aspects of our lives. 'How long will you refuse to keep my commands and my instructions?' (16:28) Then he explained, 'Bear in mind that the Lord has given you the Sabbath; that is why on the sixth day he gives you bread for two days' (16:29).

The Hebrew word 'Shabbath', of which this is the first occurrence, means 'to cease' or 'desist'. The sabbath was of God's making. As we read in Genesis 2:2, having completed the work of creation, 'on the seventh day he rested from all his work'.

To what extent this seventh day of rest had been observed by the patriarchs is not known, and certainly the conditions of slavery the people had been in would account for their failure to maintain it. But at this early point it was brought into Israel's practice and from then on every seventh day was one of rest.

Soon afterward a commandment by God to set aside one day in seven which would be holy, and provide rest and recreation for his people was proclaimed at Sinai. It formed an integral part of the covenant God made with Israel. In contrast to the incessant daily grind under slavery, the Sabbath was a day of release and joy to the people when work had to be kept to the minimum and the enjoyment of God and his goodness at its maximum.

Moving through the wilderness of Sin the people turned inland and arrived at a place called Rephidim in the wilderness of Sinai. Once again the water supply was a problem and the people accused Moses of bringing them out of Egypt only to destroy them by thirst in the wilderness (17:3). God commanded that he should take his staff with which he had once struck the river Nile turning its waters to blood, and strike a rock so that water would gush from it.

The stream of water that resulted met their needs and once again it showed the care God had for them. Rephidim was close to Mount Sinai whose slopes probably extended to it. It is possible that the water from this rock continued to flow and that the children of Israel obtained their water supply from it while they camped on the Sinai Plain for the next year. The record in Psalm 105:41 states: 'He opened the rock, and water gushed out; like a river it flowed in the desert.'

It was here at Rephidim the Israelites had to fight their first battle (17:8). They were attacked by Amalekites, a roving people who were destined to become perpetual enemies until they were finally wiped out in the reign of Hezekiah hundreds of years later.

Already the Amalekites had tried to hinder Israel on the escape journey by attacking the weak and the stragglers at the end of the column (Deut. 25:17, 18), but this time the attack was in the form of a pitched battle.

Moses appointed Joshua to gather together a body of fighting men. His task was a difficult one. The enemy were seasoned fighters but the Israelites, recently released from years of bondage, had no military experience and would have few weapons available.

However, victory was not dependent on these factors—it was in the hand of God. Moses climbed a nearby hill with that same staff which God had already used in a remarkable way, and there he prayed. When his hands were raised in supplication, Joshua's troops advanced; when he let down his hands the Amalekites gained ground. But fortunately Moses had with him his brother Aaron, and Hur (whom Josephus says was the husband of Moses' sister Miriam). These two men held his failing arms upright, and as the sun set, the battle was finally won and the people of Amalek mown down with the sword.

Being by this time in the wilderness of Sinai, Moses was on his home ground because it was in this region that he had spent forty years of his life after fleeing from Egypt. Here he had been married, and from here God had called him as he tended his father-in-law's sheep in the vicinity of Horeb. At Rephidim Moses was visited by Jethro, his father-in-law, who brought with him Moses' wife Zipporah and his two sons Gershom and Eliezer.

When he observed how overworked Moses was, his father-in-law suggested that an organisational structure of the families be introduced by which there would be rulers over tens, fifties, hundreds and thousands. Rushdoony points out that 'since the basic governmental structure of Israel was by families (and hence by tribes of families), it is safe to conclude that the tens refer to ten families. For each ten families one judge was appointed to deal with minor matters and to refer other cases to a higher jurisdiction.'* Moses welcomed this process of delegating responsibility and after seeing it successfully in operation Jethro returned alone to his own country.

*R. J. Rushdoony *The Institutes of Biblical Law* p. 313 (The Craig Press).

2 | THE COVENANT

The Israelites moved on and three months after the exodus reached Mount Sinai where they encamped on the plain that stretches before it. Sinai, identified as the mountain now known as Jebel Musa, was some 2,200 metres high and the people were to stay on the plain beneath it for another nine months. It was to be one of the most important periods in the entire history of the Jewish people for during it they received the revelation of God's law and the way of approach to him in the sacred Tabernacle.

The first communication from God to the people at Sinai was a spoken one. But before God spoke he required two days of preparation on the part of the congregation. They had to realise that God would not speak casually and that there must be a period of consecration preceding the sound of his voice. After the grime and dust of the journey there had to be cleansing in those two days and all their clothes had to be washed. Even their married lives must be held in abeyance as their hearts and minds were prepared to hear God speak.

Moses drew a boundary at the foot of the mountain beyond which no person or cattle might pass on pain of death. And when the third day dawned there were visible and audible signs coming from the mountain which caused fear and trembling in the camp (19:16).

A thick cloud settled on the hills and one peak became the object of intense thunder and lightning with an enormous blast as of a trumpet constantly sounding out from it. This was the prelude to God speaking to his people and the sign for Moses to bring them out of the camp so that they might meet God (19:17).

Thousands moved towards the boundary line. In horror they watched the mountain as though it had turned to fire with the smoke of the fire ascending as from a furnace. At the same time it was shaken by a violent earthquake and the trumpet blared louder than ever. At God's command Moses once more issued a warning that no one should attempt to cross the boundary of the consecrated mountain.

Then God spoke. He spoke not only to his servant Moses as had happened previously, but to the whole congregation (20:1, 19; Deut. 5:4, 22). In place of the trumpet the people heard the very words of the Lord, although they did not see the speaker.

What they heard was the Decalogue or Ten Words which we refer to as the Ten Commandments. One after another, in the most awe-inspiring setting, God made known the basic principles governing man's relationships to him and to his fellow men. They were not the threatening precepts of a judge but the wise counsel of a father.

Nevertheless, by the time God finished speaking the people were so terrified that they begged Moses to intervene and communicate God's words to them instead. When they heard the voice of God they feared death, and asked Moses to go forward into the darkness and from then on he alone heard the voice of God which he later communicated to the people (20:19, 21; Deut. 5:5).

What Moses then received from God were the laws and the covenant enacted between God and his people. The record of these laws is contained in more than three chapters of the Bible (20:22–24:4). It is referred to in Scripture as the 'Book of the Covenant' and covers such subjects as laws relating to the altar, slaves, murder, civil offences, property rights, social duties, ethics, and many others.

When Moses returned to the congregation he recounted to them all the words of the Lord and the various ordinances (24:3). They, in turn, freely pledged their obedience saying, 'Everything the LORD has said we will do.'

The next day (24:4ff.) was one of the most important in their history for in it they ratified a covenant with God. This has been singled out as the day on which these motley people really became a nation. They had received a divine revelation and they responded to it by entering into the binding covenant God offered them.

At this point we must turn from the actual events as they happened at Sinai in order to consider the nature and significance of that divine covenant which was of the greatest importance in the history of Israel.

A covenant is an agreement between two or more persons and Scripture mentions several made between man and man, such as Jacob and Laban, and David and Jonathan. But the really important covenants were those made between God and man.

That kind of covenant was unlike a human agreement in which the contracting parties approached each other on a somewhat similar level. In the divine covenant God was always on a higher level reaching down to make an agreement with mankind, entirely as an act of grace. His covenant was a purely voluntary promise, though it generally contained certain conditions for its fulfilment, either stated or implied.

The first covenant he made was with Adam in the Garden of Eden (Gen. 2:17), it was followed by one with Noah (Gen. 6:18), another with Abraham (Gen. 12:2), later again with David (2 Sam. 7:16). The one God initiated at Sinai is generally referred to as the Mosaic Covenant (Ex. 19:5).

The fact that God established a formal covenant with the children of Israel immediately after their escape from Egypt was of great significance. They were a weak and demoralised people but God offered to weld them into a powerful theocracy—a nation ruled over by God himself.

The Lord would exercise his government for the most part through men whom he would raise up and give to the nation, but he himself would at all times be Head of the nation. His presence would be central in the Most Holy Place and in him all the powers of statehood—legislative, executive and judicial—would be united.

It is helpful to analyse the Mosaic covenant because it introduces for the first time a particular pattern or form in its make-up. In this way it is similar to the written suzerainty treaties or covenants in existence amongst the Hittite people during the period 1400–1200 BC which was the time of the exodus.

A suzerain, or sovereign-ruler in those days, would

dictate an agreement to his vassals which normally had six elements, every one of which is paralleled in the Sinai Covenant.* It is significant that God should employ a form which was in contemporary use and would be readily understood by the leaders of the people.

1. Such a covenant always commenced with the *preamble* which identified the author of the treaty. A typical introduction from an archeological find commences, 'These are the words of the son of Mursilis, the great king, and king of the Hatti Land, the valiant, the favourite son of the storm god ...' In contrast, the preamble identifying the author of the Covenant with Israel had a simple dignity, 'I am the LORD your God' (20:2).

2. The second element of a suzerainty treaty was the *historical prologue*. At this point in the Hittite covenant the suzerain reminded the vassal ruler of the benefits that had been conferred on him by the sovereign ruler and this formed the basis of the vassal's gratitude and future obedience.

At Sinai the historical prologue simply added the record of God's goodness to his people in these words, 'who brought you out of Egypt, out of the land of slavery' (20:2).

3. The third stage of a covenant stated the *stipulations or obligations*. One contemporary Hittite covenant does this by saying, 'But you Duppi-tessub remain loyal to the king of the Hatti land ... Do not turn your eyes to anyone else.'

God at this stage in his covenant says, 'You shall have no other Gods before me. You shall not make for yourself an idol in the form of anything in heaven above or on the earth beneath or in the waters below. You shall not bow down to them or worship them; for I, the LORD your God, am a jealous God' (20:3–5).

4. The fourth element detailed the *sanctions*, that is to say the blessings on the one hand or curses on the other which would accompany the keeping or breaking of a covenant. At this point in the divine covenant the sanctions relating

---

*See article R. Allan Killen and John Rea *Wycliffe Bible Encyclopedia* (Moody Press).

to the ten commandments included such phrases as 'punishing the children for the sin of the fathers' (a curse) and 'but showing love to thousands' (a blessing) (20:5, 6 see also 20:12; 23:20–33; Lev. 26).

In biblical covenants the confirmation or guarantee that the covenant would be kept was either an oath, or the death of the one who made the covenant. The death of the covenant-maker corresponded to the death of a testator whose will would then come into operation and therefore could never be altered.

The Israelite covenant was a sworn agreement. Deuteronomy 29:12 refers to it as 'a covenant with the LORD your God, a covenant the LORD is making with you this day and sealing with an oath'. So the parties to such a testament had to become nominally dead so that it would be just as impossible for either of them to change their minds and abrogate the covenant as it would for a deceased person to alter his will. Consequently substitutionary death actually took place and the blood of the slain animals involved was sprinkled at the ceremony when Israel ratified the covenant. Half the blood of sacrifice was thrown on the altar of the Lord and the other half sprinkled towards the people. This represented in symbolic form the 'death' of the contracting parties.

Both the ceremony and its underlying significance are referred to by the writer of Hebrews when he explains, 'In the case of a will, it is necessary to prove the death of the one who made it, because a will is in force only when somebody has died; it never takes effect while the one who made it is living. This is why even the first covenant was not put into effect without blood' (9:16–18).

5. The fifth element of contemporary covenants related to the *witnesses*. Other such treaties enlisted the names of a multiplicity of pagan gods to act as witnesses to a covenant.

In this covenant the one and only God was himself one of the contracting parties, but nevertheless, the element of witness was included. The words that Moses so carefully wrote down were themselves a witness in writing and Joshua subsequently referred to the written law as being 'a witness against you if you are untrue to your God' (Josh. 24:27). Later Moses called on 'heaven and earth' as witnesses. He said that the book or scroll of the law as it was kept by the side of the ark of the covenant would 'remain as a witness against you' (Deut. 31:26).

6. The sixth and final element of a sovereign-ruler treaty was the *perpetuation* of the covenant. In the covenants of that time the treaty documents would be safely maintained by placing them before, or keeping them beneath, the idol of a national god. The Mosaic covenant was maintained by having the stone tablets retained within the holy ark which was actually named 'the ark of the covenant' (Num. 10:33), while as we have learned, the book of the covenant was safely stored by the side of the ark.

Those tablets were more than a series of laws, they preserved the central core of the covenant between God and Israel. They were a declaration of the Lordship of God. In keeping with their suzerainty treaty or covenant purpose it is thought that 'the full covenant summary, the Ten Commandments, was inscribed on each of the two tables of stone, one table or copy of the treaty for each party in the treaty, God and Israel'.*

It was also the practice for treaties to be read in public from time to time so that the people and their children might be familiar with their terms. This was provided for by God in regard to his covenant with Israel. Before his death Moses once more recounted the statutes and laws of the covenant. Upon entering the Promised Land Joshua was responsible for a further public reading of the law and for having it recorded on plastered stones on Mount Ebal (Josh. 8:30; Deut. 27:2). In addition to this, every seven years the whole law was required to be read publicly at the Feast of Booths.

The treaty pattern which we have studied is not only evident in the events at Sinai but is clearly seen in the Book of Deuteronomy where Moses combines his farewell address with Israel's renewal of the covenant. The entire book is

---

*Meredith G. Kline *Treaty of the Great King* p. 16 (Eerdmans).

outlined by many commentators entirely within the
framework of the suzerainty covenant pattern.

The discovery that God's covenant with Israel flows
along these particular lines shows that he chose to speak to
his people in a way that was familiar to the men and
women of that day. He is a God who acts in history and
who uses the circumstances of each particular age to lead
and teach those who belong to him.

Bible scholars have also found that some of the
intricacies of the form establish the Mosaic covenant as
having been ratified before 1200 BC because subsequent
Aramaic and Assyrian treaties of the first millennium BC do
not contain a number of the distinctive elements which are
common to the Hittite and Sinai covenants.*

Our understanding of the covenantal form has enabled us
to see that the Book of Deuteronomy is much more than a
restatement of the laws given at Sinai. Its stress lies to a
greater extent upon the covenant relationship between God
and his people than upon the actual laws themselves.
Consequently, when Jesus was challenged by an expert in
Mosaic law as to its greatest commandment, he based his
reply on this covenantal relationship identifying it as 'Love
the LORD your God with all your heart and with all your
soul and with all your mind'. The legal expert agreed with
this; the relationship of love, as stated in Deuteronomy
(6:5) was indeed more important than actual legal
considerations (Matt. 22:36 ff. RSV; Mark 12:28 ff.).

But as we move on from our consideration of the
covenant significance we must always remember that while
other covenants of that age were based on power and
conquest, the covenant God made with his people was
initiated only by his love and grace towards them. He is
always a covenant-making and a covenant-keeping God.

On the day the covenant was ratified, Moses' first action
was to build a stone altar at the foot of the mountain and
erect twelve pillars, one for each of the tribes of Israel.

*See Meredith G. Kline *The Treaty of the Great King* also article 'Covenant'
Wycliffe Bible Encyclopedia.

Sacrifices were made and half the blood of the animals was applied to the altar of the LORD. This is the first record on a national basis of a practice that would form an essential part of Israel's approach to God and be more fully developed in the coming revelation of tabernacle worship.

After the sacrifice had been made Moses publicly read the entire book of the covenant in the hearing of the people. Once again they gladly gave their response saying, 'We will do everything the LORD has said; we will obey' (24:7).

This was now the second time they had confirmed their desire to be God's people. The first time had been at Sinai when God had pointed out through Moses just how he had delivered and cared for them, as though bearing them on eagle's wings. If they would keep his covenant he promised they would be his own possession among the nations, 'a kingdom of priests and a holy nation' (19:1–6). The people accepted this relationship and promised loyalty to God.

This second occasion, which had even greater significance, took place after they heard the voice of God giving his basic commandments. Then, at their request, Moses had stepped in and been responsible for communicating the more detailed terms of the covenant.

So once again they confirmed their agreement and reiterated their loyalty to God. Consequently their decision was not a hasty or unconsidered one, for the content of the covenant had become increasingly understood with time. In addition, on this occasion it was accompanied by that solemn sacrificial ceremony in which the nation made its vows to God.

Upon receiving this confirmation, Moses took the remainder of the sacrificial blood and, with a dramatic gesture, sprinkled it towards the people symbolising the covering of their sin and thereby ratifying their covenant with the Lord.

As soon as the covenant was firmly established, God called for leading representatives of the people to climb to a certain point on the mountain. Moses and Aaron then set out with some seventy Israelite leaders who crossed the boundary for the first time and ascended the hill. From its heights God gave these men a manifestation of his glory and presence in the clear blue of the sky and they ate a meal together related to the covenant made on the plain below.

When the main body returned to the camp, Moses and his servant Joshua climbed even higher. After six days Moses was called alone into a cloud that enveloped the summit of Sinai. At that moment to the people down below 'the glory of the LORD looked like a consuming fire on top of the mountain' (24:17).

For forty days he remained in the divine presence while new revelations were given him. And it is during this revelation that we first come across the word 'tabernacle'— a word which thereafter was to appear well over four hundred times in the Bible.

The record of these forty days alone with God covers seven chapters of the Book of Exodus (25–31). Throughout this period Moses was given instruction by God on how men should approach him. Legal and ethical teaching was absent. The whole concentration was upon the way by which God's people might draw near, starting with the point at which a sinner could receive forgiveness and proceeding to that unique meeting of God and man in the Most Holy Place on earth.

When Moses waited in the glory of God's presence to receive his commands he did not know what possible warnings or admonitions lay ahead. But when God spoke it was to tell his people that with willing hearts they should give their possessions for his service; everyday material things freely offered so that worship of a unique pattern might be made possible. It is remarkable that such a great and impressive happening should yield a simple request from the Almighty for the material things of life to contribute to a structure that would show man how he might approach God in his holiness.

'Tell the sons of Israel', said God, 'to raise a contribution for me; from every man whose heart moves him you shall raise my contribution. And this is the contribution which you are to raise from them: gold, silver and bronze, blue, purple and scarlet material, fine linen, goat hair, rams' skins dyed red, porpoise skins, acacia wood, oil for lighting ... And let them construct a sanctuary for me, that I may dwell among them' (25:1–8 NASB).

There could scarcely be a greater contrast than the display of God's power and glory which surrounded Moses on the one hand and his call for man's giving on the other. It is a call which is just as relevant today to each of God's people for as Jesus said, 'Freely you have received, freely give' (Matt. 10:8).

This clearly showed that the God of Israel was not a God who would remain remote from his people, dwelling in unapproachable majesty like the gods whom others worshipped in fear and trembling. The God who spoke to Moses was a personal God vitally concerned in the lives of his people and seeking their involvement in his worship, even being willing to accept their material offerings in his service.

There is no thought here of a Superior Being who disdains matter because it is tainted and evil—a concept that was to become prevalent in non-Christian religion. Here is a good and holy God who is the creator of matter, and wants to see it offered willingly in his service so that it will glorify him.

Furthermore he is a great God who asks great things from those who can give them, but will receive with equal joy small things from those who are limited by their means or ability. From some he might ask the gift of gold, from others simply bronze. One may be able to bring the fine linen of Egypt while from another he will be pleased to receive a gift of goat's hair. One man is asked to give silver but from another God only seeks some olive oil. He is an understanding God, reading the hearts of those who bring their offering and not compiling a schedule of values. He is the God who watches a woman drop two copper coins into the temple offering and says to his disciples, 'I tell you the truth, this poor widow has put more into the treasury than all the others. They all gave out of their wealth; but she, out of her poverty, put in everything—all she had to live on' (Mark 12:43).

But notice what God says to Moses after he has asked for the gifts of those who love him. He states the purpose of his call for hearts to be moved saying, 'Then have them make a sanctuary for me, and I will dwell among them' (25:8).

Such is the purpose of the gifts. They were to be used in making a building to be set apart for the worship of God. But after revealing that the gifts were for a sanctuary, God goes much further and discloses the unique purpose of this sanctuary. It is that 'I will dwell among them'.

This was truly an amazing revelation, that the Lord God Almighty was proposing to make his presence known, not only from the heights of heaven or even the far off summit of Mount Sinai, but that he wanted to dwell down in the camp among his people.

This is the uniqueness of the one who had revealed himself to Moses as Yahweh, the self-existent, the one who is because it is his nature to be. But he is also an essentially personal God acting as redeemer of those other persons—his own people.

The wonder of the true God is that he seeks to form a living and a loving relationship with men and women, the relationship of father to son or daughter. He takes the initiative in bringing this about, an initiative which was to reach its fulfilment in his coming to dwell among mankind by way of a stable in Bethlehem.

So the people who had been overwhelmed by fear at the evidence of God's presence as they had seen it on the mountain were soon to learn that they would not have to experience him at a distance in a state of terror. He would take his place in the very centre of the camp and would lay out a pattern by which they could be at peace.

Hundreds of years later King Solomon continued to be amazed at the thought that God was prepared in some way to presence himself with humanity. He asked, 'But will God really dwell on earth with men? The heavens, even the highest heavens, cannot contain you' (2 Chron. 6:18).

When God said to Moses, 'Have them make a sanctuary for me, and I will dwell among them,' he did not leave it to Moses or Aaron or the council of seventy elders to devise a sanctuary worthy of his presence for he immediately continued, 'Make this tabernacle and all its furnishings exactly like the pattern I will show you' (25:9).

The materials might be provided by God's people but the plan would belong entirely to God himself. Man could not think up or institute his own way of approach to a holy God. Nevertheless, God in his grace was willing to formulate a way by which man with all his imperfections could approach God and have the assurance that God dwelt with him.

In every detail the building thus set apart had to conform to the divine pattern and it is when we examine this pattern that we can see how God planned the way of approach to him. We know that like the tabernacle itself it was temporary. It was designed to meet the needs of his people at that particular moment in history.

The tabernacle was made from materials which would pass into obscurity. Physically, none of it would remain in recognisable form but the pattern is eternal and the wonderful thing about the tabernacle is that it still communicates to us the way in which sinful man can make his approach to an altogether holy God.

God unfolded that way of approach. Moses could never have thought it out for himself; the mind of man dared not conceive it. Only God could chart the way. But even though this way into God's presence was revealed a thousand and more years before Christ, it is quite remarkable how it points in one way after another to him who declared; 'I am the way and the truth and the life. No-one comes to the Father except through me' (John 14:6).

Emil Brunner has stated 'The understanding of the Old Testament is the criterion and basis for understanding the New'. Consequently as we study God's tabernacle revelation it is not an academic consideration of a discarded way, but it is an attempt to understand better a fulfilled way; a way that was accomplished by God himself in Jesus Christ.

As we have seen, when God first spoke to Moses his words related to an offering (NIV) or contribution (NASB) which everyone who had a willing heart should make towards the construction of this place of worship. Then he stated his purpose; to make it possible for him to dwell among men.

But when God begins to disclose the divine plan and pattern which will embody that purpose, we find that he begins at the Most Holy Place of all, giving the specifications of a piece of furniture which is to be more sacred and unapproachable than any other.

'Have them make a chest of acacia wood' (25:10) are the first words he speaks in the unfolding of his plan. This chest or ark, unique amongst the furnishings of God's house, was so holy that even to touch it brought immediate death to the man who had not been accepted by God for this purpose (2 Sam. 6:7).

We notice that God begins his revelation at the point of ultimate objective. God starts where he is to be found and then his instructions work outwards from the Most Holy Place, through the Holy Place into the outer court, until, at the very entrance gate God designates the place where sinful man may first approach him—at the sacrificial altar.

The divine principle is to begin with the heart of God's purpose, the ultimate truth that there is a place where man can enter God's presence and be accepted by him. There is a point at which, under carefully regulated conditions, a man may enter the Holy of Holies. There he will find himself in the presence of that infinitely Holy Being whom Nehemiah speaks of as 'the great, mighty and awesome God' (9:32), while Samuel asks, 'Who can stand in the presence of the LORD, this holy God?' (1 Sam. 6:20).

The Shorter Catechism of the Westminster Divines starts at the same point and asks in question one, 'What is the chief end of man?' and responds 'Man's chief end is to glorify God, and to enjoy him for ever'. It begins, as it were, in the Holy of Holies, in the place where it has been made possible for man to form a vital relationship with God through which he can glorify him and enjoy the favour of the Almighty. And it is not until we come to the eighty seventh question that its compilers ask, 'What does God require of us, that we may escape his wrath and curse due to us for sin?' There we have come to the place of human repentance, redemption and faith in Jesus Christ. Such is the altar of sacrifice at the entrance to the tabernacle.

When we, as sinful men and women ourselves, study the meaning and purpose of the tabernacle we start where man begins in all his imperfection, taking those first faltering steps toward God.

3 | REBELLION AGAINST GOD

Just how sinful the human heart is was demonstrated once again even while Moses was communicating with God on Sinai. By the end of those forty days the whole tabernacle pattern had been made known by God in very clear and specific directions. Two stone tablets with the basic ten commandments engraved on them had been handed over to the Israelite leader and he was ready to return to the people with the great news that God was willing to dwell among them.

But tragically, at that moment God was obliged to speak to Moses in words that swept away his joy at the things he had been learning. 'Go down, because your people, whom you brought up out of Egypt, have become corrupt. They have been quick to turn away from what I commanded them and have made themselves an idol cast in the shape of a calf. They have bowed down to it and sacrificed to it and have said, "These are your gods, O Israel, who brought you up out of Egypt"' (32:7, 8).

It was the worst moment of Moses' life. Worse by far than that day when he had been forced to flee from the court of Egypt to spend forty years as an exile in a foreign land. It was worse than the desperate days in which

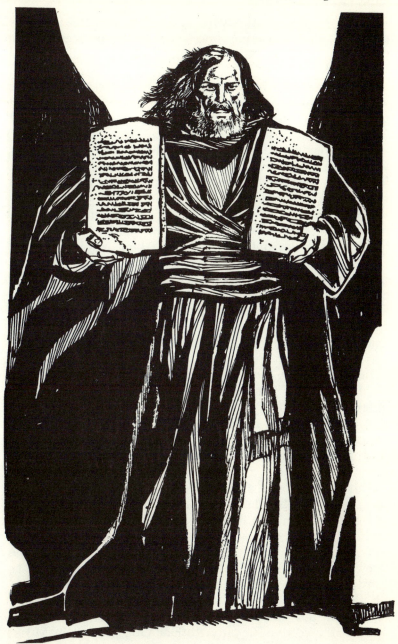

Pharaoh resolutely refused to free the people. It was worse even than that shattering time when the people accused him of bringing them out of Egypt simply to die in the wilderness and stated their preference for slavery.

It was worse by far than any of these. Moses could cope with ingratitude, criticism and antagonism towards himself as leader. But he could not bear open rebellion against Yahweh, the redeeming God of his people.

Moses recognised how angry God was with the Israelites who had so recently accepted the solemn covenant with all its implications, but had now repudiated the compact and the God with whom they had made it.

And here we see Moses at his greatest. From the mountain top God disclosed that he was ready to sweep into oblivion the sinful covenant-breaking masses of Israel and make a fresh start to build a whole people for himself based upon Moses as founder and head. We cannot envisage just what such a thing meant to a man of the ancient world. To be offered the glory of a whole nation which would emerge from his family line, to be appointed a leader under God of an entire people consecrated to him was an honour unequalled in history.

But Moses put God first. The name of God meant more to him than the name of Moses the son of Amram, and he interceded for the people with the Lord. He presented a most reasoned argument in favour of sparing the existing nation. He sought to avoid any lessening of respect for God on the part of the surrounding peoples, and asked God to take account of his former close relationship with Abraham, Isaac and Jacob. By his effective intercession for the people on the plains he disbarred himself from one of the greatest honours that had ever been urged upon any man.

When God broke the news of the rebellion to Moses, he knew that on the plains the people had rejected him as Lord and the words he spoke reflected this. 'Go down,' he said, 'because *your people* ... have become corrupt' (32:7). He did not speak of them as 'his people' for they had cut the cords of loyalty to their God. But when Moses rejected all preferment for himself, he showed his determination to bring these rebellious people back into their covenant relationship with God when he asked, 'Why should your anger burn against *your people?*' (32:11)

Moses loved the people and he longed that they should always be held in the hand of God. That is why in his response, he brought them back where they belonged, into the keeping of Yahweh when he referred to them as '*your people*, whom you brought out of Egypt with great power and a mighty hand' (32:11). And what happened next is beautifully stated in the words of Psalm 106:

> Praise the LORD.
> Give thanks to the LORD,
> for he is good;
> his love endures for ever.
>
> At Horeb they made a calf
> and worshipped an idol cast from metal.
>
> So he said he would destroy them—
> had not Moses, his chosen one,
> stood in the breach before him
> to keep his wrath from destroying them.
>
> But he took note of their distress
> when he heard their cry;
> for their sake he remembered his covenant
> and out of his great love he relented.

That is what happened between God and Moses while the most unsavoury things were happening on the plain.

Moses then took the two tablets of the testimony (the decalogue) in his hands. Contrary to the practice of the day they had been engraved on both sides but contrary to any form of writing known by man, 'the tablets were the work of God; the writing was the writing of God, engraved on the tablets' (32:16). God's servant began the descent of the mountain and was rejoined by his assistant, Joshua.

As they neared the lower slopes, Joshua was dismayed by the sound coming up from the camp. He turned to Moses and as a military commander would, interpreted the shouting of the people explaining, 'There is the sound of war in the camp.' But as Moses listened he caught the strains of something more ominous and replied, 'It is not the sound of victory, it is not the sound of defeat; it is the sound of singing that I hear' (32:18).

As they pressed on to see what was really happening they found the people engaged in an orgy of dancing and merriment with a golden calf as the centre of their activities. In hot burning anger and before the eyes of the watching people who with amazement saw their leader reappear, Moses cast the stone tablets from his hands and smashed them at the foot of the mountain of God. His indignation was justified. The people had already annulled their covenant with God so he broke to pieces the central body of that covenant.

The Israelites had become tired of waiting. They had watched as Moses with his brother Aaron and the seventy elders had ascended the mountain. After a time Aaron and the elders had reappeared and taken their place in the community, but Moses was still on the upper reaches of Sinai as it towered fearsomely above them.

The mountain was stark and barren and as day succeeded day all hope that Moses would return safely began to fade. As they spoke about Moses they began to refer to him as 'this fellow Moses who brought us up out of Egypt' (32:1). This was in marked contrast to the song of Moses who, on the western bank of the Sea of Reeds, had rightly ascribed that action to God:

'I will sing to the LORD, for he is
   highly exalted.
The horse and its rider he has
   hurled into the sea.
The LORD is my strength and my song;
   he has become my salvation.
He is my God, and I will praise him,'
                    (15:1, 2)

Moses was in no doubt that it was the LORD who had brought them up out of Egypt by his mighty hand, but the people had transferred their confidence from God to the servant of God and had come to regard him as the one they could not do without. It is an error made by many of God's followers to this very day.

While the Israelites recognised that Moses was great enough to have an understanding of the unseen God, they had begun to feel the need of a god whom they could see with their own eyes, and who could visibly go before them on the march. 'Come, make us gods who will go before us,' was the demand they made to Moses' brother Aaron.

'What did these people do to you?' asked the baffled Moses of his brother, 'What did these people do to you, that you led them into such great sin?' (32:21)

He knew that Aaron's heart really was with God, but somehow the people must have exerted unforeseen pressures

31

to have him make a golden bull calf as an object of worship. But at the same time Moses placed the responsibility where it lay; on the shoulders of the man who had been acting as leader and his words to his brother were most solemn, 'You led them into such great sin'.

Aaron had yielded to circumstances, he had compromised in a situation where his own faith in God pulled him one way but his fear of the people drove him along the path of expediency. Even when he was saying to the people, 'These are your gods, O Israel,' he was, at the same time, proclaiming that the feast where the golden calf was central would nevertheless be in honour of the Lord. 'Tomorrow', he said, 'there will be a festival to Yahweh'* (32:5). Well, Aaron might designate it as such, but Yahweh would not be present.

Moses was burning with anger as Aaron attempted to justify the middle course he had steered. On the one hand he had debased the glory of God into the image of a bull and on the other had involved this animal thing in a futile attempt to honour the Almighty.

'Do not be angry, my Lord,' he pleaded with his younger brother and explained how he had asked the people to provide gold which they were already displaying on their person. But in keeping with the self-justification of the man who has been disloyal to his Lord, Aaron finished his defence with one of the most unconvincing and indeed nonsensical explanations that could possibly come to mind. 'Then they gave me the gold, and I threw it into the fire, and out came this calf!' (32:24) It seems that the man who departs from the Lord must resort to ludicrous explanation for doing so.

When Moses looked at the people he saw that they were quite out of control (32:25) in a way which would make them the laughing stock of their enemies. He knew that this was not the moment for a carefully reasoned speech telling the people how they had erred, trying to persuade them to discard their idol, admit their folly and turn back to God in

*or, the LORD.

repentance. He knew that the whole process had gone too far for any such approach and that the only thing to do was to make a dramatic call for a decisive commitment to God by those who had no wish to be associated with idolatory. He also knew that, tragically, the only thing to do with those who were committed to the bull calf as their god was to excise them like a malignant cancer from the body of Israel.

Moses took up his position at the entrance to the camp and cried, 'Whoever is for the LORD, come to me.' It was the descendants of Levi who turned their backs on the heathen worship that had been so utterly ineffective in Egypt. They rallied to God's representative in answer to his call that they should declare themselves to be God's men.

They were the people who must purge sin in the camp. Acting on Moses' instructions they armed themselves with swords and moved from one side of the camp to the other executing vengeance on the idol worshippers. They could spare neither neighbour, brother or son until the work of judgement was completed. By the end of that tragic day some three thousand men suffered the ultimate penalty of sin—death.

For their loyalty to God and his servant, for their fearless obedience in the execution of judgement, the Levites were given a unique blessing in the purpose of God. For having proved their devotion to Yahweh Moses announced, 'You have been set apart to the LORD today ... and he has blessed you this day' (32:29).

The entire tribe was, as a consequence, set apart as dedicated people to carry out duties connected with priestly rites and functions. The priests themselves arose from the family of Aaron who like his brother Moses was a Levite, but from this moment on the Levites became the favoured tribe to assist in every phase of the work of God.

Later when the tabernacle was built they served the priests who were in attendance there and assisted them at the altar. They looked after all the materials and were responsible for transporting them on the long journey to the Promised Land. No one else could handle the fabric or furnishings of the sacred structure, on pain of death.

When the people of God encamped on their travels the Levites were allotted a special position surrounding the tabernacle. The other tribes were placed beyond them at a greater distance from the holy house of God. The Levites were its special protectors and ready to give their lives in its defence.

But those who had survived the sword still had to face an unpleasant reminder of their sin. Moses took the offensive bull image, associated with the fertility bull-cults of Egypt, and had it melted down. It was then ground to powder and mixed with the drinking water. Then the people had the unpleasant experience of drinking their own sin and at the same time received an object lesson in the total inability of any man-made object to come to their aid. Indeed it may actually have led to a harmful plague which then took its toll of the people (32:35).

On the following day Moses spoke to the congregation about the seriousness of their sin and told them that he would once more have to beg God's forgiveness on their behalf (32:30). This meant yet another climb into the higher reaches of Sinai where he would seek some way by which their sins could be atoned for.

In the presence of God, acting as mediator on behalf of the twelve tribes of Israel, Moses first of all confessed their sin. What he had told the people on the plain, 'You have committed a great sin', he now confessed to the one they had offended, 'Oh, what a great sin these people have committed!' And then he went further and designated their wrongdoing, 'They have made themselves gods of gold' (32:31).

The progression is interesting and instructive to us. It was of course God who had acquainted Moses with the people's sin before his servant even knew about it. Nevertheless, in coming to seek atonement, the 'at-one-ment' of those who were at variance, Moses took nothing for granted. He followed out the principle of confessing one's sin exactly as the Apostle John stated in his epistle (1 John 1:9).

First of all on the human level, down on the plain, there

had to be recognition of sin. This is exactly what Moses, as their spokesman, confirmed when he told them, 'You have committed a great sin'. John saw this primary need for us to face up to our wrongdoing when he stated, 'If we claim to be without sin, we deceive ourselves.'

But recognition of sin is not sufficient. It must be followed by confession in line with John's direction beginning, 'If we confess our sins.' In the presence of God Moses was very specific. He could have reasoned that it was God who first informed him of Israel's transgression and it was therefore unnecessary to designate it. Moses did not, however, try to avoid the embarrassment of being altogether honest about the failure of his people for, in words which must have been painful for him to frame, he said to God, 'They have made themselves gods of gold.' It was exactly as John put it, 'If we confess our sins'.

'Our sins'—they must be brought before God in all their unpleasantness; the actual, designated, stated sins by which we have offended against him. Of course he knows them already, but if we seek to be 'at one' with him we must be open and frank as we ask for his forgiveness (1 John 1:8, 9).

Moses had a greater understanding of God in his holiness and supremacy than any living man. He knew that the sin of the people could not have reached deeper than it had done. It was a solemn thing to break a treaty with God, but it was completely abhorrent to replace the Almighty with a metallic bull. All sin is offence against God, but to depose God is the terminal sin. 'I am the LORD,' he says, 'I will not give my glory to another or my praise to idols' (Is. 42:8).

Moses understood that to gain forgiveness for this offence was beyond anything he could expect. Nevertheless he approached God. He began to put it into words and got so far as to say, 'But now please forgive their sin—' Then he stopped. It was asking too much. It was beyond possibility. He never completed that sentence. Instead he did one of the most wonderful things in his life. He interposed himself between God and the people, offering to be the sin-bearer upon whom God's righteous judgement would fall. 'But if not,' he continued, 'then blot me out of the book you have written' (32:32).

Moses was actually offering his life as a substitute for the life of all who had sinned against God. He was asking to be destroyed in place of his people—not merely to be put to death but to suffer eternal separation from God by being blotted out of his book. Moses who had mediated as a spokesman was offering himself now as a mediator to be an atoning sacrifice for sin, if such should be possible.

It was not. Blotting the name of their leader out of the book of life could never take away the sin of others. Not even the sacrifice of so great a man as Moses could be effective for this. Every man must die for his own sin; 'Whoever has sinned against me I will blot out of my book' (32:33). However, God in his mercy was soon to describe a way by which that sin could be covered over until a new 'Moses' would arrive on the world scene—one who was himself without sin—and who would do for the covenant community what this willing man had been unable and unworthy to achieve.

4 | RENEWAL OF THE COVENANT

After the rebellion had been put behind them God told Moses that the people could continue their journey. Although they did not actually move for many months, they did have the Lord's gracious promise to assist them to their destination rather than abandon them as a result of their rebellion against him.

At this point in the biblical narrative we are introduced to what is called a 'tent of meeting'. We first learn of it in Exodus 33:7 where it says, 'Now Moses used to take a tent and pitch it outside the camp some distance away, calling it the "tent of meeting".'

Although the tabernacle in all its glory is also referred to as a 'tent of meeting' we must not confuse the two. They were both tents in which the purpose was that God would meet with man, but this tent of meeting could never fit the description of the ultimate tabernacle. The critics waste a great deal of time and effort trying to explain away a disharmony of their own making.

The tent of meeting was essentially a very simple erection and stood in marked contrast to the elaborate

tabernacle. No request for materials to make it was ever recorded nor is there any suggestion that it had any form of ornamentation. The only attendant associated with it was Moses' own assistant, Joshua, not any of the priests.

Moses took this tent (before the construction of the tabernacle was begun) and pitched it 'outside the camp'. It stood well away from the camp because God had for the time being withdrawn his presence from those who lived there. As they saw Moses' action, the people learned the lesson that their sin in the camp had separated them from God. When the tabernacle was built, however, it would be central in the camp and subject to the divinely regulated manner of approach to him. God would 'dwell among them' (Ex. 25:8, Num. 2:1ff.).

When Moses went out to the tent of meeting to talk with God the people realised that this was a solemn moment. They stood at the doors of their tents keenly watching him until he went inside. Then the pillar of cloud descended and they knew that their leader and protector had entered the presence of the Lord.

While Moses was hidden from sight every man standing by his tent joined in worship (33:10). But within the tent of meeting the relationship between God and the man Moses was so unique that the record says, 'The LORD would speak to Moses face to face, as a man speaks with his friend' (33:11). This direct revelation was later reaffirmed by God when Moses was under severe criticism from those closest to him. God overwhelmed the critics when he designated his unique relationship with Moses in these words:

'When a prophet of the LORD is among you,
I reveal myself to him in visions,
I speak to him in dreams.
But this is not true of my servant Moses;
he is faithful in all my house.
With him I speak face to face,
clearly and not in riddles' (Num. 12:6).

But Moses had a problem, and he brought it to God who alone could resolve it. God had ordered that the people must, in due course, move on from Sinai and go northwards to occupy the land which he had promised to Abraham, Isaac and Jacob saying, 'I will give it to your descendants' (33:1). However he had recently stated that he could not go with them lest his judgement on their obstinacy would result in their destruction (33:2).

So Moses placed his difficulty before the Lord in words like these (33:12): 'You have been telling me, "Lead these people," but you have not let me know whom you will send with me. You have said that I have found favour in your eyes.' Now this was good, but Moses needed something more. To lead these people through everything that lay ahead he needed the assurance that he would be taught the way of God.

He prayed, 'If I have found favour in your eyes, teach me your ways so that I may know you' (33:13). And God replied, 'My Presence will go with you, and I will give you rest' (33:14).

God's presence might have been removed for a time from the masses of Israel but it would always remain with his faithful servant Moses. With the perpetual presence of God in his life he would be at peace, and his mind at rest. This rest that God promised him would not mean freedom from worry, strain, danger, criticism, weariness, discouragement and a host of other problems, but it did mean that in the turmoil of life the presence of God would give him an enduring peace within. He would know that God was with him and, as he carried out the will of God, he would experience that calmness and assurance which can only be found when life is lived under God's control.

So when Moses heard that wonderful promise of God, 'My Presence will go with you, and I will give you rest,' he added his joyful 'amen' in these words of confirmation: 'If your Presence does not go with us, do not send us up from here. How will anyone know that you are pleased with me ... unless you go with us? What else will distinguish me and your people from all the other people on the face of the earth?' (33:15, 16).

And Yahweh responded, 'I will do the very thing you have asked, because I am pleased with you and I know you by name' (33:17). To know a man by name meant, in the language of that day, to know the whole man; to have a deep understanding and communion with the whole person. This was the depth of relationship God forged with Moses. He offers it to us through Jesus Christ who, in his coming said, 'My sheep hear my voice and I know them, and they follow me.'

But Moses had one more longing. God knew Moses; but how very much Moses longed to know God! Encouraged by the gracious words that the Lord had spoken to him the Israelite leader made a request that has no parallel, Moses said, 'Show me your glory' (33:18).

What Moses longed for was to see more of God than had ever been revealed. To be given a sight of the very nature of God. To have a manifestation of the sum of God's attributes. And God replied, 'I will cause all my goodness to pass in front of you, and I will proclaim my name,

Yahweh*, in your presence' (33:19).

Moses had asked to see the 'glory' of the Lord but what God promised Moses was a sight of his 'goodness'. How perfectly the two are brought together in the divine character. Men may have a measure of glory without goodness but in our God his very goodness is his glory.

'And', God continues, 'I will proclaim my name Yahweh,* in your presence.' He had ended his previous sentence by saying to Moses, 'And I know you by name.' Now he offered to proclaim to Moses more of the wonders of his own name—that is, of his character—so that Moses could experience an even greater disclosure of the divine Person.

It was in the vicinity of Sinai that God had first revealed to Moses some of the wonders of his character as exemplified in that name. During the years of obscurity Moses was keeping the flock of Jethro his father-in-law when he led them to the far side of the desert and came to Sinai. A bush which was on fire but did not burn up attracted his attention and he went to investigate. Suddenly he was stopped in his tracks by the voice of God telling him to come no closer because he was on holy ground.

Speaking from the heart of the flames, God had called Moses to the task he was now carrying out. He not only promised to be with him but to give him a sign by which he would receive confirmation that all he had done had been the work of God. He said, 'I will be with you. And this will be the sign to you that it is I who have sent you: when you have brought the people out of Egypt, you will worship God on this mountain' (3:12).

No more than one year later God's sign had been fulfilled. Though the path had not been easy, Moses had come to the place where God told him he would return, doing exactly what God had said he would do.

As the bush burned that night Moses had a particular concern that worried him. He put it to the Lord in these words, 'Suppose I go to the Israelites and say to them, "The God of your fathers has sent me to you," and they ask me, "What is his name?" Then what shall I tell them?'

**or, the* LORD.

God replied, 'I AM WHO I AM. This is what you are to say to the Israelites: "I AM has sent me to you"' (3:14). That formula, 'I AM' when used in the third person became Yahweh, 'HE IS'.

Yahweh is the most significant name for God found in the Old Testament—the name in which the subject does not become an object but remains subject. It is the personal name for God, a proper noun. Yahweh is quite distinct from the general term 'God' which might, in the use of language, be applied to a completely false god. There could, however, be only one Yahweh for he is a personal God entering into every man's life.

The name means, 'he which is' or 'he who is truly present', and that name was a promise to Moses that the Lord God was the actively present one. He would be present with Moses as leader and with his people as he redeemed them from bondage.

Thus for Moses there was the goodness of God to be seen and the name of God—his essential character—to be understood. These were the things Yahweh promised him in a personal encounter which would give him the strength to go forward and also provide the evidence he needed of God's favour.

Returning to Mount Sinai we find God's response to Moses' request was qualified, 'You cannot see my face, for no one may see me and live' (33:20). To see 'the face' of God would mean seeing God himself. God uses the term 'my face' and 'me' interchangeably and the glory of God is so overwhelming that no man could bear the sight of it. To see God face to face would mean knowing him absolutely, plumbing the depths of his being and would result in the destruction of a man.

Therefore, God picked out a place on the mountain where the rock was cleft and Moses sheltered in it. In a theophany (an appearance of God to man) he passed by the place where Moses stood, though the man's vision was temporarily obscured for his own protection. After God had passed the restraint was removed and Moses saw all that he could bear of the wonder of the Lord. He saw the afterglow of the Almighty and that was as much of God's glory as any man could possibly endure.

Moses' previous experience on Sinai had resulted in the breaking of the covenant tablets. They lay in fragments at the foot of the mountain. When God spoke once more to this spiritually renewed man, Moses heard words of divine grace that brought new hope to Israel. 'Chisel out two stone tablets like the first ones, and I will write on them the words that were on the first tablets, which you broke. Be ready in the morning, and then come up on Mount Sinai. Present yourself to me there on top of the mountain' (34:1, 2).

These words brought a ray of hope to Israel even though there was no promise attached to them. Moses, who had recently asked so much of God, did not enquire further.

With a sense of expectation he prepared the stone tablets, declared the holy mountain out of bounds to man and beast, then rose early in the morning, 'and went up Mount Sinai, ... as the Lord had commanded him' (34:4). His was the obedience of faith and hope in a God of love.

Ascending the great hill Moses reached the heights where thick cloud obscured everything around him, and in that cloud God spoke. Would Moses learn anew of the righteousness of God, of his judgement on all who sinned, and would they be stern words of warning? No! When God spoke, he spoke of mercy and grace and steadfast love and faithfulness. God spoke of himself.

'And he passed in front of Moses, proclaiming, "The LORD, the LORD, the compassionate and gracious God, slow to anger, abounding in love and faithfulness, maintaining love to thousands, and forgiving wickedness, rebellion and sin. Yet he does not leave the guilty unpunished"' (34:6, 7).

Moses bowed to the ground and worshipped God, thoughts of his greatness and mercy flooding through him. Encouraged by God's response he said, 'O LORD, if I have found favour in your eyes, then let the Lord go with us. Although this is a stiff-necked people, forgive our wickedness and our sin, and take us as your inheritance' (34:9).

Apprehensively Moses waited to hear God's response to his plea. Could the Lord forgive the people for rebelling against him? As they stood at that moment they were a weak and helpless people. Without a sovereign-ruler covenant they must either perish in the wilderness or make their way back to Egypt and submit to Pharaoh as dejected slaves.

And God said, 'I am making a covenant with you' (34:10). So it was true! His mercy and grace and steadfast love and faithfulness were true and in this moment reaching out to the undeserving. God was willing to start all over again and make a renewed covenant with his people. Indeed, he continued, 'Before all your people I will do wonders never before done in any nation in all the world. The people you live among will see how awesome is the work that I, the LORD, will do for you' (34:10).

So God renewed the covenant. And when he did, he came to this people as to no other people on earth and made them the hub of history.

In the renewal he summarised much that he had previously stated and added further warnings and instructions. One was especially apposite, 'Be careful not to make a treaty with those who live in the land where you are going, or they will be a snare among you' (34:12). God in his grace was bringing a second covenant into existence but there must never be a competing covenant in their history, there must only be one sovereign-ruler; God himself.

This principle still stands for us today. Our God has brought us into a special relationship with himself. He has brought us into his own family and we must acknowledge no other lordship but his, and contract no spiritual loyalties other than those entered into with him. As Jesus said, 'No-one can serve two masters ... you have only one Master' (Matt. 6:24; 23:8).

Moses was with the Lord for forty days and wrote on the tablets the ten commandments of God. To his astonishment when he returned to the camp the people were once more filled with fear when they saw him—but this time for a very different reason.

It was not their leader's anger with their sin that terrified them, but it was the radiance of his person that filled them with awe. Here was a man who had lived so close to God that something of the divine presence remained with him as he came back to the community. Here was a man who had begged God, 'Teach me your ways, so that I may know you' (33:13), and who, in his deepening knowledge of the Eternal, had ultimately asked, 'Show me your glory'. Here was a man who had caught a vision of the Infinite and when he stood among the people he radiated the wonder of knowing God. When the record says that 'the skin of his face shone' (34:29 RSV) it uses an unusual word that would be better translated as his skin 'shot forth beams'.

The people had to avert their eyes at this phenomenon

while the reflection of God's glory still radiated from the face of Moses. They turned away but Moses called them to come back and listen to the words God had spoken again on Sinai.

After he had finished giving them God's revelation he was obliged to place a veil over his face so that those who looked at him would not be overwhelmed. But when he went in to speak with God, the veil was removed for, in the divine presence, nothing must come between God and man rather it should be that the reflected glory is enhanced.

Paul wrote of this in his second Epistle to the Corinthians and when he referred to this event related it to the experience of the person who has communion with God through Christ. 'And we, who with unveiled faces all reflect the Lord's glory, are being transformed into his likeness with ever-increasing glory, which comes from the Lord, who is the Spirit' (2 Cor. 3:18). It is God's purpose that his glory should not only be reflected by Moses, but by all who have come to know and love God.

5 | PREPARING FOR THE TABERNACLE

At this point we must go back to that earlier time when Moses spent forty days alone with God on Sinai, to the first words God spoke, 'Tell the sons of Israel to raise a contribution for me' (25:1, 2 NASB). Then he followed this request with the detailed plan of a tabernacle and its furnishings which set out the pattern of approach by man to God. All this had been sadly interrupted by the rebellion of the people when they broke their sovereign-ruler covenant.

As chapter 35 opens, we find that after the traumatic experiences of the last few weeks Moses has been able to bring the people back to the place of offering their goods and services with willing hearts in the building of the holy tabernacle.

In chapters 25–31 Moses had been given the actual pattern of the tabernacle together with detailed instructions regarding its materials and furnishings. Those seven chapters dealt with commands which originated with God, but the remaining chapters 35–40 are a record of the previous commands being put into effect. Consequently, from this point on we will be dealing with the design and construction, the purpose and significance of the tabernacle and all that related to it.

The tabernacle which God planned was essentially a portable worship centre. Whenever God moved, his people had to be sure that they moved with him, so it was designed for mobility and ease of transportation.

It was not God's plan that the inspired simplicity of the tabernacle should be superseded by the grandeur of a static building such as the temple, though he permitted Solomon to do so. It is significant, however, that in his defence before the Sanhedrin council Stephen argued that God's true pattern of worship was found in the simplicity and mobility of the tabernacle, and not in the static temple. And even in Jerusalem that temple itself was quite often referred to as the 'Tent' or the 'Tent of Meeting' (1 Chron. 9 *et al.*).

The word 'tabernacle' has become enshrined in the English language to describe this divinely appointed place of worship. It simply comes from two Hebrew words '*ōhel* and *mishkān*' which mean 'tent' and 'dwelling'. They designate a tent in which the Lord was willing to meet his people—a movable sanctuary. Sometimes referred to as 'the tabernacle' and at others as the 'Tent of Meeting' it is also spoken of as 'the tabernacle of the Testimony' and 'the LORD's house' (see Ex. 36:8; 35:21; Josh. 6:24). Another translation is 'the Tent' or 'the Tent of the LORD's Presence' or 'God's Tent' (see Ex. 35:11; 36:21, GNB; 2 Chron. 1:3).

There is significance in the fact that the Almighty God chose to be worshipped in a structure so ordinary as 'a tent'. Although in the first instance this was suited to the local conditions He continued to regard this simple and movable structure as the ideal pattern for a worship centre. Wherever his people went it accompanied them and his presence could be recognised among them.

Later when David was struck with the idea that this form of tent inadequately expressed the glory of God he was made aware of God's thoughts by the prophet Nathan. 'This is what Yahweh* says: Are you the one to build me a house

*or, the LORD.

to dwell in? I have not dwelt in a house from the day I brought the Israelites up out of Egypt to this day. I have been moving from place to place with a tent as my dwelling' (2 Sam. 7:5, 6).

To discover the primary objective of the tabernacle we go back to God's words when he said to Moses, 'Then have them make a sanctuary for me, and I will dwell among them' (25:8).

A sanctuary is a place 'set apart' for the worship of, and communion with God. The first reference to a 'sanctuary' comes in the praisegiving song of Moses after the escape from Egypt. There he refers to it as 'the place, O LORD, you made for your dwelling' to which he will bring his redeemed people and reign over them as king (15:17, 18). Such is the ultimate sanctuary, it is the reality which lies ahead of God's people, and of which any earthly sanctuary, and the tabernacle especially, is but a foreshadowing.

On Sinai God had set out a pattern of law which he knew man would not be strong enough to keep. In fact as Paul said, 'through the law we become conscious of sin' (Rom. 3:20).

But equally, on the mountain, God offered a remedy to the person who 'becomes conscious of sin'. He showed Moses a way of forgiveness for the repentant sinner. It was forgiveness gained at the cost of a living sacrifice which opened up the way for the sinner's representative to enter the presence of God on his behalf.

Many years later the Apostle John was to write, 'For while the law was given through Moses, grace and truth came through Jesus Christ' (John 1:17 NEB). Only through Christ could the demands of the law ever be satisfied. Only by him would the full effects of grace be experienced in the life of a sinful person. But until that day, God gave his grace in measure by providing a way of forgiveness in the tabernacle pattern.

When we come to study this pattern in greater detail there are certain excesses which we must avoid. One is to regard the tabernacle merely as a localised portable sanctuary belonging to a nomadic people which had no relevance beyond the forty year period of wilderness wanderings. The opposite extreme is to allegorize the details of the tabernacle structure and furnishings. In this way we can become so immersed in spiritualised meanings and fanciful interpretations which have no scriptural warrant, that we lose sight of the greater wonder of God's grace as revealed to Israel and to us.

An allegory involves the use of language to convey a deeper and different meaning from that which appears on the surface, and we will certainly find deeper meaning as we study the tabernacle plan and its furnishings. But an allegorical interpretation gives to each detail in a story or situation a distinctive meaning, or makes it represent some particular truth of its own. The danger with allegory (which is very sparingly used in Scripture) is that the interpreter is tempted to attach to any part of the tabernacle structure a meaning which its Designer never intended. In this connection the reformed theologians, who largely rejected allegorical interpretation, adopted instead the principle that we must 'not carry a meaning into but draw it out of the Scriptures'.

We would do well to try and maintain this criterion as we proceed to study some of the details of the tabernacle, and not to carry our own meaning into the item under consideration but to draw out of it a meaning consistent with Scripture.

It might be helpful to illustrate this point by giving two examples of different writers using the allegorical method. Referring to five wooden bars that ran horizontally round the structure of the building, one says that with five being the number of 'grace', these bars represent the grace of Jesus Christ binding his children together.*

Pick up the next book and the reader will find the author saying that these same objects represent the five church ministries of apostles, prophets, evangelists, pastors and teachers.†

---

*Jones, Glenn M. *Big 10 Tabernacle Topics* (Moody Press).
†Flack, A. J. *Tent of His Splendour* (G.L.S. Bombay).

That second writer says that the five pillars of the front entrance door represent Christ's incarnation, life, death, resurrection and exaltation. But dealing with these identical pillars the first writer has them representing Paul, John, Peter, Jude and James.

There are, of course, no valid explanations given by either writer why these five bars and pillars should have that particular significance attached to them. On this principle of biblical interpretation any other writer is quite free to come along and place an entirely different meaning on the same items. This kind of interpretation is nothing but personal assumption and individual conjecture. It is, in fact, a manipulation of the text.

This brings us to a more appropriate method of biblical interpretation known as 'typology'. The term is derived from the Greek word 'typos' meaning 'pattern' or 'figure'. In Romans 5:14, for example, Paul explicitly describes Adam as 'a pattern (or type) of the one to come', that is, Christ.

It is always possible for typology and allegory to overlap, but typology is much less speculative than allegory. A 'type' has been defined as 'an event, person or object which by its very nature and significance prefigures or foreshadows some later event, person or object'.*

Types always originate in the real and historical and they are prophetic in nature, pointing forward to what is to come. They are all directed towards Christ himself or that which arises through the coming of Christ. Types are not afterthoughts which we read back into the earlier events in the Old Testament, but they can be recognised as having been inherent in the earlier event.

As an example of the correct interpretation of a type let us think of the lamb which the Israelite offered as a sacrifice for the sin he had committed (Lev. 4:32).

Many years later that lamb could be recognised as being a 'type' of Jesus Christ for it pointed forward to the one whom John the Baptist distinctly identified as, 'the Lamb of God, who takes away the sin of the world!' (John 1:29)

*D. F. Payne *New Int. Dictionary Christian Church.*

The error of a type becoming an afterthought which the interpreter reads back into the earlier event would happen if we considered the first miracle of Jesus, by which he made water into wine.

Should we then think back into the Old Testament where there are many references to wine and say, 'This means that wine is a type of the miracles Jesus would perform', we would be guilty of reading a type back into an earlier event without any scriptural assumption.

We must, of course, accept that the significance of any type in the Old Testament might not be apparent until the 'antitype' or fulfilment had been recognised. An example of this is Jonah's experience which Christ used as a 'type' of his own resurrection.

Broomhall has stated that, 'Much of the Old Testament (for example Ex. 25–40) would have only antiquarian value today if it were not for types embedded in the text.'*

Their use falls into two categories. There are those of which the interpreter can say, 'This is a type of such-and-such', because the Bible designates the one as being a type of the other. We have seen this as between Adam and Christ. Then there are those which are not identified in the Bible text as types, but which the interpreter may, with care and discretion, regard as being so.

In this study we will, to a considerable extent, avoid the term 'type' and rather enquire to what extent the event, person or object is an illustration of a divine truth anticipating a fuller revelation in Christ. The words of Pascal in his *Pensées* sound a warning here, 'He who will give the meaning of Scripture, and does not take it from Scripture is an enemy of Scripture.'

In the case of the tabernacle and its pattern of approach to God we are, however, on firm ground in regarding it as a type of what is to come. The New Testament book of Hebrews makes this explicit. Referring, for example, to the necessity for shedding blood in the tabernacle ceremonies, it states: 'It was necessary, then, for the copies of the heavenly

*Wick Broomhall *Baker's Dictionary of Theology*.

things to be purified with these sacrifices .... For Christ did not enter a man-made sanctuary that was only a copy of the true one; He entered heaven itself' (9:23, 24). In that passage the tabernacle is distinctly referred to as 'a copy' of that which came through Christ. Thus we have the tabernacle referred to as 'a copy' of that which came through Christ—in fact a type!

Again in Hebrews 8:5 we are told about the service of the priests on earth and it is stated, 'They serve at a sanctuary that is a copy and shadow of what is in heaven.' Note the expression, 'a copy and a shadow', in other words a type of the final reality.

In Hebrews 9:9 referring to the actions of the High Priest on the annually repeated day of atonement in the tabernacle, the writer declares, 'This is an illustration for the present time, indicating that the gifts and sacrifices being offered were not able to clear the conscience of the worshipper.'

So we have biblical authority for a typological interpretation of this subject which presents numerous 'copies, shadows and illustrations' of what is to come.

It is also interesting to find that when John speaks of Christ in the prologue to his gospel he says; 'The Word became flesh and lived for a while among us' (1:14) and uses a Greek verb corresponding to the noun 'tabernacle' so that his statement literally declares 'The Word became flesh and tabernacled (or pitched his tent) among us'.

The building of God's Tent in a wilderness by people so recently subjected to bondage was a magnificent achievement. The skilled craftsmanship required was of the highest order in a structure to be filled with the presence of God. And God had his particular man ready for the task.

The Lord said to Moses, 'See I have chosen Bezalel ... of the tribe of Judah, and I have filled him with the Spirit of God, with skill, ability and knowledge in all kinds of crafts' (31:1ff.).

The name 'Bezalel' means 'in the shadow of God', and the man who has lived his life close to God is the man he can use. So God called him by name, just as he had called

the man of his choice from the burning bush by name—
'Moses, Moses'.

Something essential happens in the life of the person who
responds to God's call. The Lord said of Bezalel, 'I have
filled him with the Spirit of God'. This comes before any
artistic or natural ability anyone may have. In fact the
greatest need in God's service is to be filled with the Spirit
of God. Hundreds of years later Paul was still echoing this
truth when, writing to the church in Ephesus which also
lived in the shadow of one of the most magnificent
buildings in the world, he stated their priority in life, 'Be
filled with the Spirit' (Eph. 5:18). The natural talent of any
person will only be fully used by God if it is exercised by
one who is 'filled with the Spirit'. On the other hand, those
who may not possess uncommon gifts can nevertheless do
outstanding work for God if, in their lives, they are Spirit-
filled Christians.

Beyond this filling, Bezalel had some very special abilities
which were God-given. They make a most impressive list:
skill, ability, knowledge, craftsmanship, making artistic
designs, working in gold, silver and bronze, cutting and
setting stones, woodworking and all kinds of craftsmanship
(see 31:2–5).

Bezalel was not a priest, but his work was of the highest
value in the service of God and shows us that those whose
calling may be in a craft, a trade, a profession, a business
are just as much called by God to their task as are those
who work full time in his service.

Bezalel was given an assistant named Oholiab and a
number of able men to help in work which covered a wide
range of activities, from the construction of a portable
building, crafting beautiful gold work, weaving immense
curtains, making priest's clothes, down to the pressing of oil
and blending of incense.

Their gifts were varied. But as Paul tells us for our day,
'God gives his gifts to each man, just as he determines' (1
Cor. 12:11). And the principle which was so important in
the building of the tabernacle is still as vital in the building
of God's church, for Scripture tells of some twenty spiritual

gifts that God gives to his people for this task.

Bezalel was not only a craftsman, he was also the chief instructor for the project. He himself had outstanding qualifications but he could not carry out the whole tabernacle task. He therefore taught others how they could best use the abilities they had been given. '(God) has given him ... the ability to teach others' (35:34). Paul urged this principle on the church when he instructed Timothy, 'And the things you have heard me say ... entrust to reliable men who will also be qualified to teach others' (2 Tim. 2:2). And that one command marks out four generations of teachers—'me, you, reliable men, others!'

Under Bezalel's leadership were thousands of unnamed men and women whose hearts and spirits were filled with a sincere desire to play some part in this great work. There was a spontaneous movement to become involved. We read, 'And everyone who was willing and whose heart moved him came and brought an offering to the LORD for the work on the Tent of Meeting, for all its service, and for the sacred garments' (35:21).

Here we have the Spirit of God entering into their leader, and the human spirit of each of these men and women reaching out to God with a desire to serve him. In Romans Paul says that the '(Holy) Spirit himself testifies with our spirit that we are God's children' (8:16), and this double operation, that of God's Spirit and man's spirit, was working in the wilderness for God's glory.

In addition to the silver half shekel head tax which was required of all males twenty years old and more (38:25–28) we read that 'all who were willing' (35:22) brought their brooches and ear-rings, rings and ornaments, all kinds of gold objects, gold itself, precious materials and fine linens, skins, silver and bronze until the point was reached where the call had to go out to stop.

What a remarkable moment this was! The hearts of the people so overflowed with love that Moses had to command throughout the camp, 'No man or woman is to make anything else as an offering for the sanctuary' (36:6).

Should we wonder how these ex-slaves came to possess

such rich goods the reason is that when tragedy struck the Egyptians they could not do enough to get the Israelites out of their land. God had already instructed that, in compensation for their suffering, the Israelites should ask for silver and gold and had promised that his people would not leave Egypt empty-handed. So what they were now giving freely to God was the reward they had received for years of labour. It was a real sacrifice but 'everyone who was willing and whose heart moved him' brought his offering to God with joy.

6 | THE CONSTRUCTION OF THE TABERNACLE

When we turn to the tabernacle structure we must first of all look at the tent itself, the main feature in the complex. It was an oblong structure measuring thirty cubits in length and ten cubits in both height and breadth.

If we enquire what a cubit is we will discover that it is the distance between the tip of the middle finger and the point of the elbow. But if we take the next step and ask whose middle finger and whose elbow? we will have to admit that we don't know. It was subject to variation since the measurement was related to different people.

The variation is estimated at between 43 to 53 cm so that we may think of a cubit as being approximately half a metre. This could mean that the central structure was 15 metres long and 5 metres in height and breadth.

The first essential of the central tabernacle was the framework on which a series of hangings would be placed to form the completed tent. To build up this portable structure it was first necessary to make 48 upright supports each of which was ten cubits (5 metres) long by $1\frac{1}{2}$ cubits ($\frac{3}{4}$ metre) broad. The wood was acacia, a tree that flourishes in

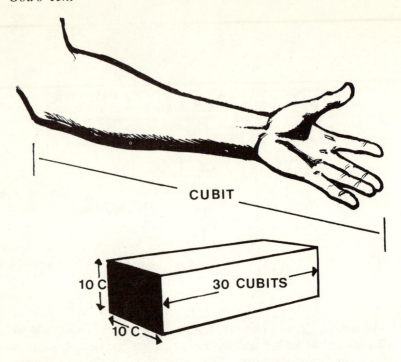

barren regions and which is still common in that area. It is very hard, browny-orange in colour, and throughout the centuries down to the present time has been used for cabinet-making.

Some translations refer to these uprights as 'boards'. The NIV and others, however, use the translation 'frames' thus: 'Make upright frames of acacia wood for the tabernacle. Each frame is to be ten cubits long and a cubit and a half wide' (26:15,16). The original Hebrew word *qereshim* has been found on a Canaanite tablet describing the 'throne room' of the diety El which was in the form of a trellis pavilion built of frames.

The tabernacle frames were made up of two long side arms which were connected to the top, middle and base by cross-rails. Apart from the fact that the acacia trees in Sinai do not grow large enough to provide a plank three quarters of a metre wide, frames would have advantages over solid planks. They would be much lighter when erected and they would not be so liable to whip. Also, the open construction would allow the inner curtain with its fine material and figures of cherubim to be seen from inside.

When these frames were placed in the upright position there were twenty along the north side and twenty along the south, whereas the rear wall had only eight frames, two of which were used on the western corners as a form of buttress (26:22, 23). The front of the tabernacle had no frames since this was the entrance, and was supported by five pillars of acacia wood set in bronze bases (26:36, 37).

When an upright frame was placed on end it had for its foundation two bases of silver, each of which weighed about 35 kg. Each base had a mortise designed so that an extension of one side arm of the frame could fit into it in the form of a tenon. These silver bases then formed a continuous foundation around the three sides of the framework.

c

They were immensely valuable but as they supported the Holy Place and the Most Holy Place, God required that this precious metal should be the foundation for the structure. Since the silver foundation buried in the sand or earth of the wilderness could not be seen by human eyes, we might have supposed that the quality of metal would not be important. But God's purpose was that his house should have a foundation of great worth, whether or not men were able to see it.

In his work for God Paul says that like an expert builder he was laying a foundation. Then he identified the foundation, not as a pattern of belief or even the strength of fellowship one should find in the church, but in a person. 'No one can lay any foundation other than the one already laid, which is Jesus Christ' (1 Cor. 3:11). Men and women today may fail to recognize the great worth of this foundation on which their lives may be built. Hidden from human vision they may disregard the merits of so valuable a foundation, but when Jesus Christ is the basis of one's life he is a foundation imperishable, secure and immensely valuable.

Once this continuous silver foundation had been set in position, the upright frames were inserted in the sockets within each base. At this point we can envisage a series of frames held from beneath and each one pointing directly upwards on three sides of an oblong. Naturally these frames would require something to tie them together and this was provided by golden rings at the top, bottom and middle of the frame, through which supporting bars of acacia wood were inserted.

Five bars were used on each side, with the middle bar running from end to end along the entire length of one side. The other two bars relating to the top rings and those for the bottom rings ran halfway along each side (26:26–30), and in this way the wall was made rigid.

We know that what was not visible below ground level was of silver. But we should note that everything that could be seen above the ground was golden. For although a great deal of timber had been used from the acacia tree it had all been covered with pure gold.

We have already noticed that the front was not enclosed by frames but being the entrance it had five pillars overlaid with gold. Two thirds of the way into the building there was a similar construction but here only four pillars were used and these were sunk into silver bases. Subsequently, a hanging curtain would close off the entrance in front of the five pillars while inside the building there would be a veil hanging in front of the four golden pillars. This formed the internal division between the larger room which was called the Holy Place and the smaller one beyond—a perfect cube—known as the Most Holy Place or Holy of Holies (26:31ff.).

At this point we have learned about the frame of the tent, its dimensions, its materials, how it was fixed to the ground, and held together. We must now discover in what way that framework was covered over to make it into the divine Tent of Meeting.

The first covering consisted of finely twisted linen woven together with blue, purple and scarlet material. This may have been dyed linen or woven material from Phoenicia. The word for 'finely twisted' linen as given in the text is an Egyptian one. That country excelled in the production of linen and especially 'twined linen' in which every thread was twisted from many strands.

In addition this lavish curtain was decorated with figures of cherubim which were either woven into or embroidered on it. Cherubim figures were only found on this and one other curtain both of which were visible inside the two holy rooms.

Cherubim (which is the plural of cherub) were celestial beings of the angelic order in the spiritual realm. They seem to have a special association with the holiness of God. When Adam sinned cherubim were stationed at the entrance to the Garden of Eden to guard the Tree of Life. They are always the servants of God and their representation on the fabric around and above the Holy Place stresses the righteousness of God and those who serve him in his perfect holiness.

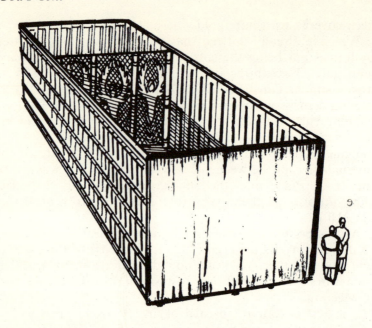

As they ministered in the Holy Place the priests saw above them and around them at all times these visual reminders of the holiness of the God they sought to honour. We too must be careful that we never let the grace of God obscure our vision of the holiness of God. We must never presume upon that holiness but live our days in the light of it. We must be obedient to it and by the help of his Spirit reproduce it in our lives.

We serve the same God whom Aaron served in the Holy Place and to him God said, 'I am the Lord your God; consecrate yourselves and be holy, because I am holy' (Lev. 11:44). And this is no less mandatory in Christ, for it was Peter who wrote to redeemed men and women, 'Set your hope fully on the *grace* to be given you when Jesus Christ is revealed ... But just as he who called you *is holy*, so *be holy* in all you do, for it is written, "Be holy because I am holy"' (1 Pet. 1:13ff.).

Strictly speaking this first beautiful covering with its cherubim formed the tabernacle. The first covering to be put over the framework was the tent itself. Referring to the method of joining this great curtain into one unit the record states that this should be done so 'that the tabernacle is a unit' (26:6). This exact use of the word 'tabernacle' should be noted because it does help to avoid confusion regarding some of the subsequent measurements, but in most other places the word refers to the whole tabernacle in the usual sense (see 25:9).

There were ten of these curtains. Each of them was twenty-eight cubits long by four cubits wide so that if we were to imagine one single length being hung over the roof and down the sides of the framework, it would hang one cubit (half metre) short of the ground on either side.

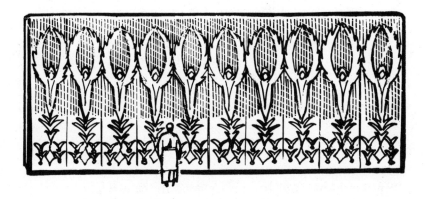

In fact they were not hung individually but five of them were joined together to make two large units, each 28 by 20 cubits. In order to couple these two sheets together fifty loops of blue thread were sewn on the side of one curtain and the same on the other curtain. Fifty clasps of gold were then used to join the curtains to one another in order, as the instructions went, 'that the tabernacle is a unit' (26:1–6).

This bringing together and making one, may remind us that this was something our Lord prayed for in the lives of his followers. It was, 'that all of them may be one' (John 17:21). Just as there must be no possibility of the separation or drawing apart of the curtains covering the holy place, so must we be obedient to the words of Scripture as given by Paul that we must 'make every effort to keep the unity of the Spirit through the bond of peace' (Eph. 4:3).

It was remarkable that at the very moment of plotting Christ's death, Caiaphas the High Priest, the only man authorised to enter the Most Holy Place should make a statement of deep significance which the apostle John describes as being prophetic. Caiaphas said that 'Jesus would die for the Jewish nation, and not only for that nation but also for the scattered children of God, to bring them together and *make them one*' (John 11:51, 52).

So in God's building there is this 'bringing together', this 'making one'. It is something very precious both to him and to us. But with all our human frailties and differences in culture, social habits and temperament it is something that we have to ensure we maintain and develop. Paul knew that there would be times when, as very human people, we would find it hard and that is why he wrote, 'Make every effort to keep the unity of the Spirit'.

Over this first tent covering there was a second tent placed which was slightly larger in size. It was made from woven goat's hair. Instead of starting with ten narrow curtains, this time eleven were used and each of them was thirty cubits by four cubits. This meant, that being two cubits longer than the linen curtain, it reached right down to ground level and entirely covered the first one.

Six of these curtains were joined to make a large unit and the remaining five to form another. The two were then united in a similar manner to the first but since this curtain was less precious than that which enfolded the Holy area, the clasps holding the fifty loops were made of bronze and not of gold.

The principle was the same throughout the tabernacle. The further one moved from the Most Holy Place the less valuable were the materials used. From gold to silver, silver to bronze, and bronze to wood. And the lesson for us is that the best must always be kept for God. He alone is worthy to receive 'praise and honour and glory and power, for ever and ever!' (Rev. 5:13).

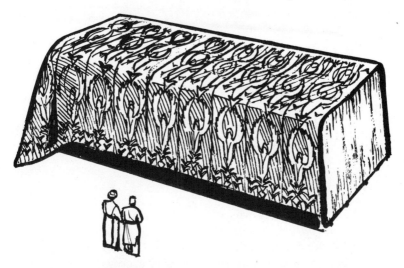

The entire length of the completed curtain, 44 cubits (18.5 metres) by 30 cubits (12.5 metres) was used for making a fold in front above the entrance (26:9) and also for overlapping the under-curtain around the sides and at the back of the tent. It also meant that the two curtains (this one and the one beneath) could be draped in such a way that their joins did not coincide.

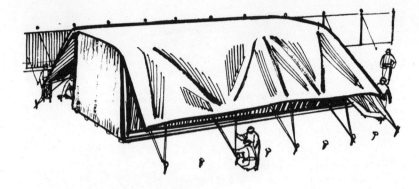

The third covering was of ram skins dyed red. It was the first of the two weatherproof coverings detailed in Exodus 26:14; 'Make for the tent a covering of ram skins dyed red, and over that a covering of hides of sea cows.' The Hebrew word '*tachash*' may refer to a porpoise or (and animal experts consider this is the more likely translation) a Dugong or Sea Cow.

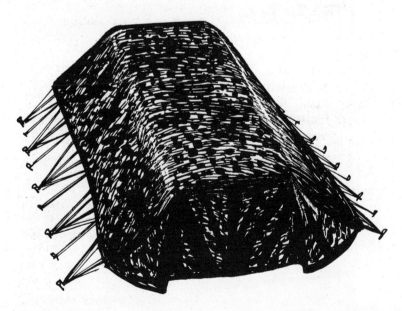

A Dugong is an aquatic mammal of about $3\frac{1}{3}$ metres long and weighs up to 300 kg. Previously found swimming along the shores of the Red Sea, it is now almost extinct. Because of the human-like breasts of the female, dugongs are probably the sirens and maidens of mythology.

Once again in the tabernacle covering there was a progression from the more beautiful to the less attractive. The first tent cover of finest white linen woven with blue, purple and scarlet and decorated with cherubim was an exquisite piece of craftsmanship. Over it hung the pleasing curtain woven from goats' hair. The next covering of ram skins dyed red had the more practical purpose of keeping the lower curtains dry. But the final cover of dugong skins, while being immensely serviceable, was far from beautiful.

Looking at this divinely ordered structure from outside it would hardly be seen as specially attractive. Only if one could gain access to the inside would its splendour and beauty be realised. It is rather like standing outside any of the great cathedrals of Europe in order to enjoy the beauty of their stained glass windows, and being disappointed at how dull and dingy, how lifeless, they appear. But enter the building and from the inside can be seen some of the most colourful and radiant art work in the world.

It was like this with the tabernacle. And in the same way there is a resemblance to Jesus Christ. The person who looks at him in a detached manner will never grasp the beauty and the wonder that resides in Jesus.

Speaking of Christ in his capacity as God's suffering servant Isaiah prophesied, 'He had no beauty or majesty to attract us to him, nothing in his appearance that we should desire him' (53:2). And this was the estimate of those who, in their day, observed Jesus and rejected him. Like the rich ruler who came close to him, but on further examination considered the glitter of his own wealth to be more attractive. King Herod and his soldiers dressed him in a beautiful robe to make him more elegant, and then observing him, considered he was only laughable. The most exclusive men in Israel saw nothing to respect in the lonely prisoner who stood before them and walked up to him pounding his head with their fists and spitting in his face.

But when this same Isaiah spoke of Christ as seen by those who had entered into an understanding of him, who had, as it were, got beneath the protective curtains and grasped something of the wonder of the Holy Person, he prophesied, 'Your eyes will see the king in his beauty' (Is. 33:17). To those who, in the words of Hosea, say 'Let us know, let us press on to know the LORD' (Hos. 6:3 RSV), an entrance is given to the Holy Place and there, and only there, can his resplendent beauty and wonder be appreciated.

7 | THE SURROUNDING AREA

Up to this point we have studied the construction and materials of the tabernacle proper. We must now move on to the whole tabernacle complex, starting with its surroundings. The building we have been considering stood in the western half of a rectangular courtyard whose dimensions were 100 × 50 cubits (46 metres × 23 metres). The tabernacle was sited from East to West with the entrance facing East.*

The outer court was enclosed by a series of curtains which were 5 cubits (2½ metres) high. The curtains were woven from fine linen and suspended from acacia wood pillars which were also 5 cubits apart. The wooden pillars each had a capital, that is to say, an ornamental top overlaid with silver. The pillars themselves were held in place by cords used as guy ropes tied to pegs driven into the ground.

Most translations refer to these upright posts as having silver fillets or bands on them, which would mean that the silver capitals were bound round by silver collars. But another interpretation is suggested in the Jerusalem Bible

*100 cubits = approx. 46   metres
  50 cubits =   23   metres
  30 cubits =   13.5 metres
  10 cubits =   4.5 metres

where we read, 'All the posts enclosing the court are to be connected by silver rods' (27:17). This would, of course, give added stability and symmetry to the linen wall.

The upright poles were each set into a socket within a bronze base corresponding in function to the silver bases beneath the tabernacle proper. This less expensive metal for a foundation indicates a third division relating to the sanctity of the tabernacle complex, the order being the Most Holy Place, then the Holy Place and now the Court of the Tabernacle.

Five separate curtains were suspended round the courtyard. Two of them ran along the long side each being 100 cubits. The one at the west end was 50 cubits long, while there were two short ones on either side of the front entrance each being 15 cubits in length.

Now this leaves a space of 20 cubits unaccounted for on the front wall just where the gate into the tabernacle was situated. In that central position there were four pillars supporting a screen made of the same material as that first richly woven curtain which was hung over the tabernacle framework. It had, however, one difference, no cherubim were represented on this outdoor screen. Cherubim were only seen within the Holy Place.

This screen with its blend of white, blue, purple and scarlet was identical to that hanging at the entrance to the tabernacle building. But it was markedly different from the plain linen screen which ran round the courtyard on either side of it. Its distinctive colouring designated the single entrance to the tabernacle area and all that lay beyond.

The plain white linen screen formed a barrier around the House of God. No Israelite could casually wander around the Holy building or stroll into the courtyard. The screen was higher than the height of a man so all that could be seen by anyone approaching this place was the top of God's Tent with the cloud that gave witness to his presence hovering over it (40:38).

The material that formed this barrier was fine white linen and the symbolism of fine linen is explained in Scripture. It comes in the Book of Revelation where, at the wedding of

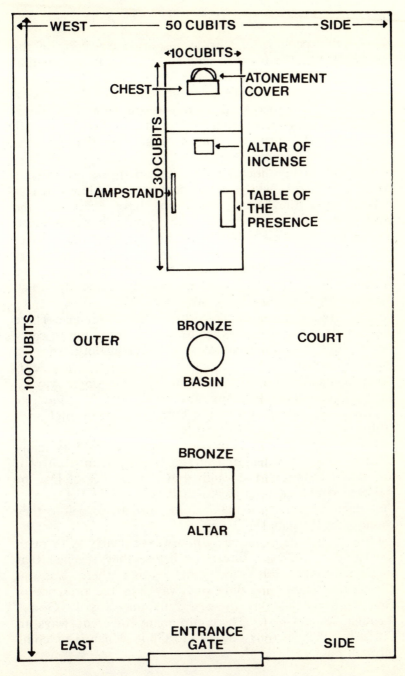

WEST ——— 50 CUBITS ——— SIDE

←10 CUBITS→

CHEST → ATONEMENT COVER

30 CUBITS

ALTAR OF INCENSE

LAMPSTAND → TABLE OF THE PRESENCE

100 CUBITS

OUTER   BRONZE   COURT

BASIN

BRONZE

ALTAR

EAST   ENTRANCE GATE   SIDE

71

the Lamb (speaking of Christ), his bride (speaking of the church) has made herself ready for the eternal union that will be celebrated between her and her Redeemer. Her wedding dress will be made of fine linen. Not silk or satin or velvet but, as we read in Revelation 19:8 'Fine linen, bright and clean, was given her to wear'. Then by way of explanation it continues, 'Fine linen signifies the righteous deeds of God's people' (NEB).

The wall of fine linen around the tabernacle presented a barrier to those whose acts were not 'righteous deeds' making sure that they would not have access to the courtyard. And, symbolically, this would have excluded every person in Israel. But as we have noticed one part of this wall was quite different. It was the 20 cubit length (9 metres) of multi-coloured curtain which designated the entrance gate. This was the one and only way by which men and women could draw near to God.

It was the single entrance to the entire tabernacle. There was no other way in. Whether he be a priest going to carry out his duties or a repentant sinner seeking forgiveness, a man had to enter by that one way. Similarly when Jesus came he identified himself as being the one single way to God. 'I am the way—and the truth and the life,' he declared. 'No one comes to the Father except through me.' (John 14:6)

The Israelite in the camp could reach this gate by many different ways. The children of Judah camped in front of it and could go straight through. But the families of Dan or Reuben would have to make their way along the side of that linen barrier, then make a 90° turn twice before they could enter the gate.

Others, such as Benjamin, could weave their way through the camp in different directions before they reached that single entrance. But the point is that there was no alternative. There was only one way into the presence of God. And in this day there is only one way to God—through Jesus Christ. There are many different ways to Christ but there is only one way to God—which is to 'come through him'.

There is also significance in the position of the tabernacle in the nation. It was central. All the tribes of Israel encamped around it and faced toward it. The former tent of meeting which the tabernacle replaced had been pitched well away from the camp area. Its purpose was only temporary. But when a way was established in which God would 'dwell among the Israelites and be their God' (29:45), he wanted his presence and his worship to be central. That is why the tabernacle was located in the middle of the camp and the people lived around it on every side.

It is still the purpose of God that he should be central in the lives of his people, and it was Jesus who promised, 'Where two or three are gathered together in my name, there am I in the midst of them' (Matt. 18:20 RSV). On the night of his resurrection he penetrated the locked doors and appeared in the midst of his disciples. 'He stood among them and said, "Peace be with you!"' (John 20:19). And only if Christ has the central place in our lives will we know that peace and assurance which reaches out from him to us.

Each of the twelve tribes had a designated area of the camp to live in. When their forefathers had moved south to Egypt many years before they had done so as a family of twelve households, each headed by one of the sons of Jacob, later renamed Israel. In Egypt they preserved these family divisions and over the years the families of the twelve sons had developed into tribes. Even beyond this there was a secondary and tertiary structure so that tribes were formed from clans and clans from families or households. That is why we read in Joshua 7:14 God commanded, 'In the morning, present yourselves tribe by tribe. The tribe that the LORD takes shall come forward clan by clan; the clan that the LORD takes shall come forward family by family; and the family that the LORD takes shall come forward man by man.'

Now although we correctly refer to the twelve tribes of Israel, we are going to find thirteen names when we identify their places in the encampment. The reason for this relates to the special privilege which was given to the tribe of Levi when it answered Moses' call to rally to him and be 'on the Lord's side', at the time of Israel's rebellion. From that moment on they were ordained for the service of God and set apart as a tribe specially dedicated to him.

This would have left only eleven tribes but the large tribe of Joseph was divided into two, consisting of the descendants of his sons Ephraim and Manasseh. Each was regarded as an individual tribe.

Not only was the loyal tribe of Levi involved in an act of dedication but also in one of substitution. On that night of terror in Egypt when the firstborn of every Egyptian family had been slain, the Israelite son lived because a lamb had died in substitution for him. As soon as this happened God called on Moses to consecrate all those firstborn sons, and those who would be born in future, to his service. They had been saved from death while those around them had died. Hence from then on, they were to be set apart for the service of God.

But when the Levites, on account of their faithfulness to the Lord, were installed as the consecrated tribe, in an act of substitution they took the place previously required of the firstborn son in each family.

Moses and his brother Aaron belonged to the tribe of Levi, the third son of Jacob. Levi had three sons; Gershon, Kohath and Merari. Moses and his brother sprang from the family of Kohath. Having chosen Moses to be leader of his people God gave further honour to the family of Kohath by selecting Aaron to be the first of his priests, and ordering that only the descendants of Aaron (prior to the institution of his church) should serve as priests and represent the people to God.

The rest of the men of Levi, known as Levites, were charged with the care of the sanctuary. This was an honourable task which no other group of people in Israel was permitted to carry out. Only the Levites could transport the tabernacle and its furnishings when the camp was on the march. When it came to rest they were the ones to erect it, care for it, and assist the priests in their work.

By virtue of their devotion to God the tribe of Levi was

allocated a position on every side of the tabernacle. Aaron, the High Priest, camped immediately opposite the entrance gate. Moses was to the north of him and Aaron's sons, the priests, to the south. Then moving in a clockwise direction the descendants of Kohath camped to the south, the Gershonites were on the west, and the Merarites to the north.

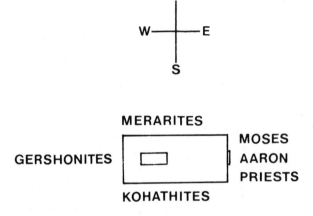

The other twelve tribes, in groups of three, had similar placings though at a greater distance than the guardians of the tabernacle. Before his death Jacob prophesied that the senior position in his family would belong to the people of Judah (Gen. 49:10) and they occupied the prime area facing the tabernacle entrance behind the tents of Aaron. To their right was the tribe of Issachar and on the other side Zebulun.

Four of the tribes, Judah, Reuben, Ephraim and Dan were recognised as tribal leaders. Each had its own standard identifying it as such while the other tribes had ensigns, a lesser type of banner. So Reuben was found immediately to the south with Gad on the right and Simeon to the left. Ephraim was central behind the tabernacle, Manasseh on his right and Benjamin on the left. The remaining tribes were situated with Dan in the centre north, Asher on the right of him and Naphtali on the other side.

ASHER   NAPHTALI

DAN

BENJAMIN   ISSACHAR

EPHRAIM   JUDAH

MANASSEH   ZEBULUN

REUBEN

SIMEON   GAD

When the time came for the people to continue their journey the signal to strike camp was given by the priests blowing an alarm on two trumpets of beaten silver. Judging from representations later found on Jewish coins and carved on the Arch of Titus in Rome, these were long straight metal tubes with flared ends about one metre long. They were quite unlike that other kind of trumpet known as a 'shophar' or ram's horn. A series of short blasts would be the signal for the tribes to move in pre-arranged order.

To the Kohathites, the first guild of the Levites, was given the task of carrying the holy furniture of the tabernacle. When camp was to be struck the dismantling and packing of these sacred objects was the task of Aaron and his sons. The Kohathites themselves were not allowed to touch the furniture or even look at it for a moment, on pain of death (Num. 4:1–16).

The object of special attention was that supremely holy article, the Ark of the Covenant. First of all the priests took down the curtain which hung between the Holy Place and the Most Holy Place and used it to cover the ark. After this it was enclosed in hides of sea cows and last of all a cloth of solid blue was spread over it. The Levites then carried it out on its poles. The other items also received three different coverings but on them the waterproof covering was to the outside. Only the holy ark was distinctive so that all the people might be able to identify it as it stood out from the rest of the sacred furnishings.

After the covering procedures were completed the Kohathites removed the various items under the supervision of the priest, Eleazer, who had charge of the sanctuary and was responsible for the Levites who worked there (Num. 3:32).

It was then the turn of the Gershonites to take over and remove the weatherproof curtains and covering from the roof and sides of the main structure together with all the hangings of the boundary wall (Num. 4:24ff.). This was done under the supervision of Aaron's son, Ithamar.

He also looked after the work of the third group, the family of Merari. They disassembled the frames of the tabernacle with its bars, pillars and bases. Then they removed all the uprights and the pegs and cords that had supported the linen screen round the courtyard.

By this time the whole community was ready to commence its journey in what was a well organised manner. First of all the Ark of the Covenant as the symbol of God's leadership was raised from the ground. The poles that ran through the supporting rings rested on the shoulders of the Kohathites who then marched at the head of the column with the ark held high (see Num. 10:33; Deut. 9:3; Josh. 3:3ff.).

In the earlier tent of meeting Moses had pleaded with God, 'If your Presence does not go with us do not send us up from here'. And God had said, 'My Presence will go with you' (33:14). The recognisable shape of the Ark of God with its distinctive blue covering gave the people of Israel assurance, that as they travelled into the unknown, God was with them, God was leading them and in his mercy would not forsake them.

This constant care and protection is not something that fell away when God's people reached the land of Canaan. It is something which the same loving, caring God has promised to his own in every generation. In Isaiah 58:8–11 we are given the assurance that God will be both behind and before us in the journey of life:

> The glory of the LORD will be your rearguard.
> Then you will call, and the LORD will answer;
> you will cry for help, and he will say: Here am I.
> ... The LORD will guide you always.

Especially meaningful to those of us who often fail the Lord is the Psalm of the Sons of Korah. Their father led a rebellion on the journey and died violently as a result. But in spite of this his sons experienced the mercy of God throughout their lives. In gratitude they sang of his care and guidance (48:14):

'...tell to the next generation. This God is our God for ever and ever;
he will be our guide even to the end.'

The symbol of God's guiding presence in those days was the Holy Ark. It always preceded the people on their journey and they knew that so long as they followed it they were going God's way. But since the coming of Christ our guidance comes from him personally. He made this plain when he described himself as the Good Shepherd 'who calls his own sheep by name and leads them out'. Then he explained that, 'When he has brought out all his own, he goes on ahead of them, and his sheep follow him because they know his voice' (John 10:3, 4).

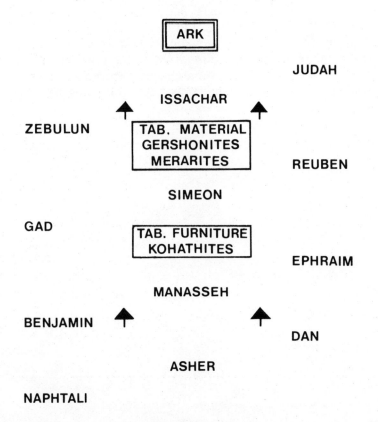

So the Israelites had the guidance of God symbolised in the Ark of his Presence, but we have God's guidance through Christ's own presence in our lives.

In the wilderness the pillar of cloud moved onwards and the Kohathites shouldered the ark as the journey began. The senior tribe, Judah, first of all took up its position and marched behind the ark on the right hand side. Following them towards the centre was Issachar and on the left, Zebulun.

Then protected by these three tribes came the Levite families of Gershon and Merari who were drawing on ox-carts all the structure and coverings of the tabernacle complex. The Gershonites were provided with two covered carts pulled by four oxen while the Merarites for their heavier load had four carts and eight oxen. They were followed by Reuben, Simeon and Gad. After them came the Kohathites carrying on their shoulders those holy articles (except the ark) which were involved in the tabernacle ritual (Num. 7:1–9). So, on the march the tabernacle furniture was central with the remaining six tribes following behind.

8 THE APPROACH TO GOD

Having seen the layout of the tribal families as they camped and the pattern of Israel on the march, we must now consider the way by which an Israelite could approach God when the tabernacle was set up.

The words of God to Moses were very specific:

> 'Speak to the Israelites and say to them: "I am the LORD your God. You must not do as they do in Egypt, where you used to live, and you must not do as they do in the land of Canaan, where I am bringing you. Do not follow their practices. You must obey my laws and be careful to follow my decrees. I am the LORD your God"' (Lev. 18:1–5).

In this instruction God looks back on the past experience of his people and refers to the time when they lived in Egypt. In spite of the amazing achievements of the Egyptian nation there was nothing in their way of approach to the deity which pleased him. His charge to the Israelites was very direct, 'You must not do as they do in Egypt'.

But then he looks forward to the land of promise where they are destined to settle and knowing the dangers of false worship there he warns, 'You must not do as they do in the land of Canaan'.

So they were in a kind of no man's land with neither the worship of the land they had left nor the one they were travelling to being in any way pleasing to God. How then could they worship him in an acceptable way?

This was exactly why they had paused in the wilderness. It was so that God could reveal his will and show them a pattern of worship that was consistent with the holiness of Yahweh yet which would make it possible for sinful man to be brought into a right relationship with him.

What was God's standard in this regard? Simply this: 'Be holy because I, the LORD your God, am holy' (Lev. 19:2). God did not lower his standards to accommodate the unworthy but he did have a plan by which his holiness could be imputed to the undeserving.

To 'impute' something to someone is to reckon it either *for* or *against* that person—it can be reckoned either to his credit or discredit as the case may be.

The principal meaning of this word is 'reckoning to the account of another'. This is what Paul asked Philemon to do with regard to the debt Onesimus had incurred, 'If he has done you any wrong or owes you anything, charge it to me' (v. 18). The word translated 'charge' is the Greek word for 'impute'.

In the life of a Christian, God carries out a work of double imputation as Paul explained when he referred to those who were reconciled to God through Jesus Christ:

> 'God made him who had no sin to be sin for us, so that in him we might become the righteousness of God' (2 Cor. 5:21).

In this way God imputed our sin to the Son and his righteousness to us.

Those who have received this double blessing should not be content to stop there. They are reminded by Peter that there should be a willing response in any life which has been so greatly blessed by God and a sincere endeavour to honour the one whose holiness has been imputed. Peter wrote, 'But just as he who called you is holy, so be holy in all you do, for it is written, "Be holy, because I am holy"' (1 Pet. 1:16).

It was in the entire pattern of tabernacle worship that God began to reveal this saving plan to men and women. It started, as it always must, with conviction of sin in the individual person's life. So when an Israelite recognised that he had sinned and this was offensive to God, and he wanted to obtain divine forgiveness he made his way to the God-appointed place, the tabernacle.

When he approached it he found that a wall of white linen formed a barrier against him. If he walked around that barrier he would find that it was 300 cubits (138 metres) in extent, but, as we have learned, there was one stretch of 20 cubits (9 metres) that was different. It was not formed of white linen but was multi-coloured in woven white, blue, purple and red. It was distinctive, and marked out the one way by which a sinner could gain access to the court of God's house.

When he passed through that entrance he found that between him and the tabernacle structure stood an altar with a priest waiting beside it.

The altar was square in shape. Its length and breadth were exactly the same as the height of the linen curtain around the court, that is to say 5 cubits (2.3 metres). Its height was 3 cubits (1.3 metres) and it was made of acacia wood sheathed in bronze with projecting horns at each corner.

Now while the English word 'altar' in our translation was formed from the Latin adjective meaning 'high' this is a late ecclesiastical derivation and not in any way connected with the Hebrew meaning. In Hebrew the word is based on a verb meaning 'to sacrifice' and 'altar' means 'a place where sacrifice is made'.

In passing we should note that as well as being a place of sacrifice it was also a place of refuge. The four horns on the corners could be used to tether animals waiting for sacrifice. But they had another use. A man who was falsely accused of murder could run there for safety and grab hold of one of these horns. If he was innocent they would protect him.

Fearing the rule of the new King Solomon, his elder brother Adonijah went and caught hold of the altar horns for safety as did Joab, David's life-long military commander (Ex. 21:12–14; 1 King 1:50; 2:28).

It is not possible to reproduce exactly the design of the Altar of Burnt Offering or bronze altar (as it was known) but a general idea can be gathered from the descriptions in the text.

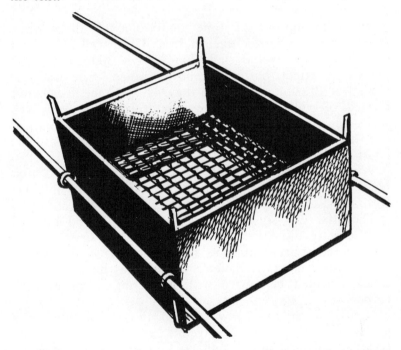

The altar was hollow so that the bronze-covered sides, 5 cubits (2.3 metres) square, contained a large area on which the bodies of the sacrificial animals could be burned by fire. There was a grating made of bronze which seems to have rested on a ledge inside the altar where the slain animals were placed and burned. It would allow the fat to drip down and the ashes to fall below. Pans and shovels were provided to rake out the area underneath the metal mesh.

There were also basins (presumably for the blood) and flesh hooks which were large bronze fork-like implements for arranging the sacrifice in order in the flames. Firepans were provided which may have been used for carrying the fire on the march.

No sin could be atoned for, neither could praise or thanksgiving formally be offered to God, without this altar being brought into use.

Every morning and evening in an act of worship a lamb was offered on the altar. On special feast days and annual rituals the Altar of Burnt Offering would be the setting for the opening acts relating to various ceremonies.

The animals to be sacrificed could vary from a young bull for the sin of a priest or the community, a male goat for the sin of a ruler to a female goat or lamb for one of the common people.

This meant that the altar might be used on behalf of the whole congregation of Israel or simply to meet the need of that one individual sinner who had found his way through the entrance screen and approached it with his unblemished sacrificial lamb to seek the forgiveness of God.

He laid his hand on the head of the innocent victim to identify himself with the one who was about to die. Then he killed the innocent lamb. The death of the lamb took place instead of the death of the sinful man. The principle was one of substitution. The sinless must die for the sinful. The blood of the blameless must be shed so that the soul of the sinner might be preserved for, 'the soul who sins is the one who will die', and 'without the shedding of blood there is no forgiveness' (Ezek. 18:20; Heb. 9:22).

At that moment the waiting priest took 'some of the blood of the sin offering with his finger and put it on the horns of the Altar of Burnt Offering and poured out the rest of the blood at the base of the altar' (Lev. 4:34). The fat of the animal was removed and burnt by fire on the altar. An atonement had been made for the man's sin and he went on his way forgiven.

The Israelite who did that had only a limited understanding of the way by which God could have forgiven his wrongdoing. But he had done something very specific which began with the fact that he recognised he had sinned and thereby created a barrier between him and God.

Making his way through the camp of Israel, penetrating the multi-coloured screen and entering the courtyard, carrying his sacrificial lamb and presenting himself to the priest as a man needing forgiveness was a *confession* of his sin. And confession or conviction of sin is always a prerequisite of forgiveness.

The next thing he realised was that he must *identify* himself with his sacrifice by laying his hand upon the lamb's head. He also knew that his sin could not be forgiven unless blood was shed. God had been very specific about that. He had stated the principle involved in the clearest terms, 'the life of a creature is in the blood, and I have given it to you to make atonement for yourselves on the altar; it is the blood that makes atonement for one's life' (Lev. 17:11).

As the blood of the lamb was shed and the life ebbed from its body the Israelite had a very real understanding of the fact that while the soul who sins will die, God had permitted the death of a lamb in *substitution* for the death of the sinner himself.

Lastly, the Israelite exercised faith that having been obedient to God's stated way of forgiveness, his sin had in fact been atoned for. God's final words to the people of Israel relating to this ritual were these; 'The priest will make atonement for him for the sin he has committed, and he will be forgiven' (Lev. 4:35). Accepting God's words by faith, this man returned to his tent believing that the barrier which had fallen between God and himself had been effectively removed.

But just how it could be removed by the life of an animal being forfeited for the life of a human was something he could not understand. He only knew that he had done what God had directed.

In the unfolding of God's revelation it later became clear that the sins of all those who had obediently sacrificed— whether as individuals or a community—had not been taken away. In that earliest written defence of the Christian faith, the Book of Hebrews, we are referred back to the sacrificial method of atonement and told that 'It is not possible for the blood of bulls and of goats to take away sins' (10:4).

And yet the record clearly stated that the sins of that Israelite had been atoned for. We may well ask why it is later said that they hadn't, in fact, been taken away?

The answer is that there is a difference between 'atonement' on the one hand and the 'taking away (or removing) of sins' on the other.

9 | ATONEMENT BY BLOOD

The word 'atonement' is one of the few theological terms that comes from the Anglo-Saxon language. In its simplest form it means at-one-ment, or a 'making at one'. It deals with the process of uniting those who are estranged, reconciling those who are at variance.

In biblical usage the Hebrew verb for 'make atonement' is 'kaphar' which means to 'cover over'. It is the word used when God instructed Noah to make an ark and 'cover it inside and out with pitch' (Gen. 6:14 RSV). That word 'cover' is the same word used in respect of the repentant Israelite of whom it was said, 'the priest shall make an atonement for him' (Lev. 4:35). So to 'make an atonement' is to 'cover' something, just as the wood of Noah's ark was covered with bitumen and could not be seen.

This means that when an atonement was made for sin at the tabernacle altar, the sin was 'covered'. It no longer formed a barrier between God and man; it was put out of the way, covered over and removed from view. But the blood that had been shed at the altar to bring about this situation was, in fact, only a symbol of the fully effective blood that would one day be shed for sin in order to 'take it away' completely. And the lamb that was slain at the altar was only a symbol, a mere shadow of the supreme sacrifice that would be necessary.

Thus it came about that when John the Baptist, the inspired prophet of God, saw Jesus he identified him in these striking words, 'Look, the Lamb of God, who takes away the sin of the world!' (John 1:29) He was careful not to refer to him as the one who 'covers up' sin. He takes it away!

Only after the coming and death of Christ did it become clear that the Israelite who had been made 'at-one' with God, had received forgiveness on the ground that he had obeyed God in presenting his sacrifice, and his sin was covered over. However, it still awaited that full and final sacrifice of the Lamb of God on the altar of Calvary before it could rightly and forever be taken away.

As the Apostle John wrote, 'You know that he appeared so that he might take away our sins' and the blood of Jesus ... purifies us from every sin'. Peter affirmed, 'He himself bore our sins in his body on the tree' (1 John 3:5; 1:7; 1 Pet. 2:24). Consequently every Old Testament sacrifice awaited the day when it would (as it were) be charged against the account of Christ's infinite sacrifice of himself on the cross of Calvary—after which animal sacrifice would forever be unnecessary.

The stress which the New Testament places on the blood of Jesus Christ as the effective means of salvation is closely related to the pattern of sacrifice instituted in the tabernacle. A scripture such as Hebrews 9:22 states the principle; 'Without the shedding of blood there is no forgiveness', while another scripture such as Ephesians 1:7 identifies whose blood has been shed to bring about that forgiveness, 'In him (Christ) we have redemption through his blood'.

One of the most significant Old Testament statements on atonement being achieved by blood is found in Leviticus 17:11; 'For the life of a creature is in the blood, and I have given it to you to make atonement for yourselves on the altar; it is the blood that makes atonement for one's life.'

This is the divinely appointed way of reconciliation between God and mankind. It is not, as some mistakenly adduce, because life exists in the blood so that a pure life is offered to God, thus making the significance of blood relate to the presentation of life.

The fact is that in the Old Testament the association of blood is predominantly with death, consequently it is by life offered up in death that atonement is effected. It is the death of the sacrifice whose blood is shed which makes it possible for the sinner to live, because God is willing to accept the death of the victim in place of the offender.

At the very beginning of his ministry Jesus was identified as the sacrificial Lamb of God who would take away the sin of the world (John 1:29). Later the apostle John wrote that 'the blood of Jesus, (God's) Son, purifies us from every sin' (1 John 1:7). Christ is the sacrifice, and according to God's edict that the blood of the substitute must be shed in the act of atonement, Christ's blood was shed when he died.

The divine principle is that the only life which atones for sin is one that has passed through death—a death in which blood must be shed—consequently Paul writing to the Romans says, 'we have now been justified by his blood' and in the next sentence affirms, 'we were reconciled to (God) through the death of his Son' (Rom. 5:9, 10). Therefore the blood of Jesus symbolises the death of Jesus, and phrases such as 'the blood of the Lamb' or 'the blood of Christ' are figurative expressions for his atoning death.

The faith of the Israelite sinner was placed in the sacrifice which was killed and whose blood was shed on his behalf. In the same way our faith must be centred in the Person of Jesus Christ who 'put away sin by the sacrifice of himself' (Heb. 9:26 RSV)—a sacrifice which involved his blood being 'poured out for many' (Mark 14:25).

When the time came for the priest who had officiated at the altar of sacrifice to enter the tabernacle proper, he couldn't do so without passing the second item of furniture, a bronze basin or laver. It was situated between the altar and the multi-coloured curtain hanging against the five golden pillars at the entrance to the building.

The bronze basin is the only item for which no specific instructions were given regarding size or shape, but it was a

bronze bowl holding water for the priests to wash their hands and feet. Every time Aaron or any of his four sons entered the court to serve at the altar they first of all had to wash their hands and feet with water from it. Every time they went to serve within the Holy Place, whether to offer incense, arrange the bread or trim the lamps, they had to wash in the same way, 'so that they will not die' (30:21).

We might wonder why washing should still be called for even after service inside the tabernacle. The reason is simple: there was no covering on the floor of the tabernacle: it was bare earth. In Numbers 5:17 there is a reference to the 'dust from the tabernacle floor'.

So we find, that, as he carried out his task in the Holy Place, the priest was surrounded above him and on all sides with the most glorious and precious materials. He was in a place where every item of furniture was either covered or made of pure gold. It was a scene of exquisite beauty in every area except one. The floor was plain earth.

From that we may understand that God made men and women to live out their lives in an earthly world. Their feet must stay on the ground and they must remain in contact with the reality of life. Even when they are in the Holy Place, involved in the service of Jesus Christ, they must never forget that their Christianity must be real and practical and down to earth. Neither must they feel that they have ever arrived at a place where they do not need to return time and time again to the basin for cleansing, to wash away the dust, even after service in the Holy Place.

The source of the bronze forming the basin came from the mirrors of women who were in the service of the sanctuary. At this stage these may have been the women who were engaged in the making of the tabernacle curtains for we are told that 'every skilled woman spun with her hands ... all the women who were willing and had the skill' (35:25).

Mirrors in those days were always made from burnished metal and no doubt at some sacrifice to themselves these women had contributed a valued item for God's service. An old Jewish writer, Aben-Ezra, said, 'It is a custom of all women to behold their face every morning in a mirror, that they may be able to dress their hair; but lo! these were women in Israel who served the Lord, who abandoned this worldly delight and gave away their glasses as a free will offering, for they had no more use of them; but they came every day to the door of the tabernacle of the congregation to pray, and hear the words of the commandments.'

The need of the priest for cleansing is one that we must equally recognise in our own lives. Even as he left the sacrificial altar to go to the Holy Place he had to wash his feet and hands in the water of the bronze basin. And we too, even though we have been to the place of sacrifice and received the forgiveness which Christ purchased for us with his own blood need to have that cleansing, that washing away of things that soil our Christian lives. As we walk through the world our feet pick up its dust. As we work in the world our hands get grimy, and we too need to return time and time again for the washing away of all that contaminates. Justification must always be followed by sanctification.

Paul recognised that Christians, those who form the church, must have a continual washing and in Ephesians 5:26 he spoke of Christ 'cleansing (the church) by the washing with water through the word'. Just as the bronze basin held water for the priests to wash in, so in the scriptures we find the cleansing we need, this 'washing with water through the word'.

It is essential for the Christian to return again and again to the word of God which will be the means of washing away so much of the extraneous matter that clings to him in this world. With pressure being applied to conform to the standards of secular society it is vital that he gets back to the word of God to find out God's standards and obey them. With error parading as truth and perversion as normality, it is essential to return to the word and ascertain absolute truth. Jesus knew this and in his last prayer for his followers asked the Father that he would keep them free from sin. 'Sanctify them by the truth;' was his request and then he added, 'Your word is truth' (John 17:17).

But if we should become careless about listening to that word of God and putting it into practice we will be like the man James speaks of when he significantly brings together the use of the word of God and the use of a mirror—and remember that the basin was made from gifts of burnished mirrors. 'Do not merely listen to the word (says James) .... Do what it says. Anyone who listens to the word but does not do what it says is like a man who looks at his face in a mirror and, after looking at himself, goes away and immediately forgets what he looks like. But the man who looks intently into the perfect law that gives freedom, and continues to do this, not forgetting what he has heard, but doing it—he will be blessed in what he does' (Jas. 1:22–25). This is how a Christian becomes 'cleansed by the washing with water through the word'.

10 THE PRIEST

The repentant Israelite who had gone through the gate of the tabernacle with his sacrifice and reached the bronze altar had proceeded as far as he dare go along the path of approach to God. Beyond that it was the province of priests to carry out spiritual tasks in the Holy Place. This they did as representatives of the people on behalf of the people. Theirs was the high privilege of the calling of God to serve him more closely than the congregation of Israel or even the specially appointed Levites could.

The general definition of a priest is 'an authorised minister of a deity who, on behalf of a community, officiates at the altar and in other rites, acting as a mediator between the deity and man'. Now that definition is applicable to all priests, even those in false religions. But when we recognise the living God as being the only deity, we can accept it as a sound definition when his name is substituted.

A priest is one who carries out sacrificial, ritualistic and mediatorial functions. This means that he is responsible for offering the divinely appointed sacrifices to God, for executing the different procedures and ceremonies relating to the worship of God, and for being a connecting link between God and man, representing the people to him.

Priest blowing silver
trumpet (*see* p. 76)

In many ways this last function shows the difference between a priest and a prophet. A priest represents the people in the presence of God, while a prophet represents God in the presence of the people.

As we have seen, the Levites were chosen as those who would specially serve God, and it was from the Levites that the priests were chosen. They originated in one family, that of Aaron and his four sons, Nadab, Abihu, Eleazar and Ithamar. But due to the unhappy deaths of Nadab and Abihu, the priestly succession came through Eleazar and Ithamar whose descendants provided the hereditary priests in Israel.

Their duties fell under three main headings. The first was to minister in the sanctuary, which at this time was the tabernacle, but when Israel became a settled nation it would be the temple. Secondly, priests were responsible for teaching the people the law of God, and thirdly, when God's will was sought for the nation, it was the priests who asked his guidance. Something of the importance of the priest in Old Testament worship may be judged from the fact that the Hebrew word for priest *'kohen'* and its derivatives occur almost 800 times in that book.

Priests wore distinctive clothing whenever they were in attendance at the altar or entered the Holy Place. Their clothing had to be clean and pure before they could approach God. A priest had linen breeches from hip to thigh. Over these he wore a coat woven in one piece with a sash round the waist and a cap covering his head. The purpose of his clothing was stated to be for 'dignity and honour' (28:40).

But the greater glory and beauty was in the clothing of Aaron the High Priest. His clothes had to be specially made by those who had been given particular ability for the task.

Over a robe of chequer work the High Priest wore a garment called an 'ephod'. It was made of linen with gold, blue, purple and scarlet, but we cannot be certain whether it was worn on the upper part of the body like a waistcoat or whether it was a kilt-like skirt.

It was intended for both the front and back of the body

and made in two parts which were clasped together at the shoulder by two onyx stones set in gold. Each of these onyx stones was engraved with names of the twelve tribes of Israel. Six names, in order of birth, were carried on one shoulder and six on the other. This meant that every time the High Priest went into the Holy Place he bore the names of the tribes before the Lord and in keeping with the character of a priest, he represented these people to God.

Over the ephod the High Priest wore a breastplate which was a pouch some 22 cm square made of beautifully woven material. On the front of the breastplate were fastened twelve precious stones in four rows of three. Once again each of these stones was engraved with the name of one of the tribes of Israel (28:21). So, with the names of God's people on his shoulders, which are associated with carrying a burden, and the names on the breastplate close to his heart we can sense something of the love and care which a priest should have for his people in the presence of their Lord.

These precious stones were set into the front of a pouch worn across the chest and attached to the ephod by golden rings. Inside the pouch were the Urim and Thummim which were used for discovering God's will.

It is not known for certain exactly what the Urim and Thummim really were, but it is thought that they may have been two precious stones, possibly gems, which were identical in shape. One or other could then be drawn from the pouch in order to provide a Yes or No answer in the quest for guidance. (See also Num. 27:21; 1 Sam. 14:41; 28:6; Ezra 2:63).

There is no record of this method being used to discover God's will after the time of David and it is assumed that with the ministry of prophets developing, the need for a more 'mechanical' type of guidance fell away. We do find a shadow of it in the action of the 120 believers who before the Holy Spirit came, prayed and then drew lots to indicate which of two men should take the place of Judas. But after the Holy Spirit was given this practice disappeared completely and God now guides his people directly by his

word and by his Spirit.

Under the ephod the High Priest wore a robe of blue. Golden bells were attached to the hem and pomegranates made from material hung like bobbles between the bells. The sound of the bells could be heard when Aaron went into the Holy Place before the Lord, and the listening people would know that he had not been struck dead in God's presence, but that his offering on their behalf had been accepted by God (28:35).

On his head the High Priest wore a turban of fine linen which bore a gold plate engraved with the words, 'HOLY TO THE LORD'. This was a constant reminder both of the status of the covenant people in Israel and of the High Priest in his calling, for the Lord said to Moses, 'Speak to the entire assembly of Israel and say to them, "Be holy because I, the LORD your God, am holy"' (Lev. 19:2). This is the essential reason that God's people should live lives consecrated to him, both morally and spiritually. Transcending every other reason for living according to the high standard of God is the reason that we love and honour a God who is altogether holy. Because this is the kind of God he is, these are the kind of people we should be.

Peter taught that the Christian's enjoyment of salvation must be followed by a life modelled on the holiness of God: 'Though you have not seen him, you love him; and even though you do not see him now, you believe in him and are filled with an inexpressible and glorious joy ... But just as he who called you is holy, so be holy in all you do; for it is written, "Be holy, because I am holy"' (1 Pet. 1:8, 15, 16).

Before any priest could take up his calling he had to go through a solemn ritual which lasted for seven days. The instructions given by God began with the statement, 'This is what you are to do to consecrate them, so that they may serve me as priests' (29:1). What follows is an act of consecration for service and to 'consecrate' means to 'set something or someone apart' for the particular service of God. The ceremony was conducted by Moses and took place at the entrance to the tabernacle within the courtyard.

First of all there had to be a symbolical cleansing, so washing the whole body was the first act. In future, as we have seen, when carrying out his task, the priest would frequently have to wash his hands and feet at the bronze basin. This reminds us of the occasion when Jesus Christ washed the feet of his followers in the upper room. When Peter remonstrated with him that it was quite inappropriate for Jesus to do so the Lord replied, 'Unless I wash you, you have no part with me.' So Peter asked him to wash not only his feet but his hands and head also. Jesus explained; 'A person who has had a bath needs only to wash his feet; his whole body is clean' (John 13:10).

The picture is that of a person returning home from the public baths, but getting the dust of the road on his feet, and only needing that to be cleansed away. Something of the same thought is contained in the fact that, at the start of his ministry, a priest had to be fully bathed day after day in a symbolic cleansing. But this would only be repeated daily in later times with regard to his hands and feet since in his holy calling he would still need (just as we do) that constant cleansing for what his hands did and where his feet went. After this the priests were dressed in their distinctive garments and their heads anointed with olive oil blended with spices (see 30:22ff.).

Speaking of the Ark of the Covenant being taken to the temple in Jerusalem many years later in Psalm 132:9 it says, 'May your priests be clothed with righteousness.' Here we have the thought that after being cleansed spiritually, the distinctive clothing should be an indication of God's righteousness, while the oil speaks of a special anointing for the service of God, an anointing which comes from the Holy Spirit himself.

At the very heart of the installation ceremony lay the sin offering. The men who would represent the people before God must first of all have their own sins atoned for. Every day for seven days they offered a young bull. As with the sin offering it had to be killed and its blood applied to the four horns of the altar before being poured out below and parts of its body burned.

A ram was then offered in an act of dedication. This was a burnt offering in which the sacrifice in its entirety was consumed in the altar flames.

Finally, every day for seven days, a further ram was offered for the priests and a distinctive ceremony attached to this last sacrifice. After their hands had been laid on it and the ram killed, Moses took some of its blood and applied it first to the lobes of the right ears of Aaron and his sons, then to the thumbs of their right hands, and lastly to the big toes of their right feet (29:20).

This act of consecration had a meaning which has lost nothing with time and should be just as real in the lives of those to whom the blood of Christ has been applied in forgiveness and cleansing. Like the priests we too must have consecrated ears to listen to the voice of God. We must have consecrated hands to carry out the work of God, and we must have consecrated feet to walk in the ways of God. Consecration to God involves the whole person.

Such was the installation ceremony of these men who were set apart for the service of God. We have seen something of their work at the altar and their cleansing at the basin before entering the tabernacle. Now we must learn what lay within that Holy Place when they entered to do the work of God there.

11 | THE HOLY PLACE

Passing through the entrance curtain into the first room of the tabernacle, the priest had at his right hand a table generally referred to as the table of the presence. It was made of acacia wood overlaid with pure gold. Its size was 2 cubits (1 metre) in length by one cubit ($\frac{1}{2}$ metre) in breadth and a height of $1\frac{1}{2}$ cubits ($\frac{3}{4}$ metre). Around the table was a border of gold and then a little further in, on the table top, an additional border which would hold the contents in place. The table had four legs, and through golden rings attached to the legs, two gold plated poles were inserted for carrying.

The purpose of the golden table was to hold twelve loaves of bread made of fine flour. They were placed there in two rows of six, each loaf representing one of the tribes of Israel (Lev. 24:8). The historian Josephus indicates that the bread was unleavened.

This bread is sometimes referred to as being the 'showbread' because in 1526, when Tyndale was translating the New Testament, he followed a German word that Luther had used to translate the phrase whose literal meaning is 'bread of the face', i.e. bread set out before the

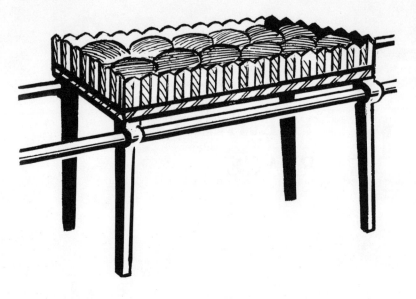

face or presence of God. It is now referred to as the 'bread of the Presence'.

It was baked from a special type of flour known as 'fine flour'. This flour was used in the preparation of food for honoured guests. Abraham had ordered Sarah to make cakes with it when he had three unique visitors come to his tent. It was the flour which was supplied to the king's. table in Solomon's reign (Gen. 18:6; 1 Kings 4:22).

Frankincense was poured on the bread as it lay there, being kept in a golden bowl alongside the table, together with other golden dishes and flagons for use in a drink offering. It was a resin obtained from Boswellia trees, one of the most highly valued incense gums with a beautiful fragrance of balsam. This frankincense constantly gave a pleasant fragrance to the Holy Place.

The cakes of bread lay on the table for seven days, then on the Sabbath day it was Aaron's duty to replace them with fresh hot bread (1 Sam. 21:6). All the priests would then assemble round the table and eat the old bread, standing in the Holy Place. For although the bread was on a table, no priest could ever be seated at that table or anywhere else in the tabernacle. Priests always stood while they carried out their duties. There was no place to be seated, no provision for rest in this pattern of worship and no suggestion that their task was ever completed.

The significance of this was very real to the writer of Hebrews when he contrasted it with the work of Christ: 'Day after day every priest stands and performs his religious duties; again and again he offers the same sacrifices, which can never take away sins. But when this priest had offered for all time one sacrifice for sins, he sat down at the right hand of God' (Heb. 10:11, 12). Only in the work of Christ as great high priest on behalf of his people was there ever finality; a sacrifice that was fully effective, a task that was completed. No priest could ever be seated but after his great cry, 'It is finished', Jesus Christ left the altar of Calvary and sat down at the right hand of God.

The fact of bread taking its place in the sanctuary was a token of God's care for his people. He was the one who constantly provided for them in their daily needs and this provision was gratefully acknowledged in his presence. It was echoed in the Lord's prayer when he said that we should ask, 'Give us each day our daily bread' (Luke 11:3). All day and every day the bread of the Presence lay on the table but it only could be 'daily bread' so long as God's presence worked in nature and provided for the needs of his children.

In time, however, his presence went beyond that and became actual in this world, not only to meet our physical needs, but to bring a solution to our moral and spiritual problems.

When he came he used this very concept of bread to describe himself. 'I am the bread of life,' he said to the crowd. 'He who comes to me will never go hungry' (John 6:35). Then he applied the figure of bread to their need of a new and eternal life. He contrasted the experiences of their forefathers who had died in the wilderness with the provision of 'the bread that comes down from heaven, which a man may eat and not die'.

He spoke of the fact that he himself was that bread and that he would give his whole self as a sacrifice so that those of us who receive him as the living bread may have eternal life. His words speak for themselves and fulfil every meaning inherent in the bread of the Presence as it lay in the Holy Place. 'I am the living bread that came down from heaven. If a man eats of this bread, he will live for ever. This bread is my flesh, which I will give for the life of the world' (John 6:51).

The Holy Place where the priests set out the bread of the Presence was a room 20 cubits long by 10 cubits wide and 10 cubits in height (9 metres × 4.5 metres × 4.5 metres). Its sides were formed by the golden upright frames through which the beautiful linen curtain with its pattern of cherubim could be enjoyed. The wall in front of the priest was of the same curtain broken only by four golden pillars that came down from a ceiling of the identical pattern. But nowhere in that sacred room was there any window or place to let in the light. It was lit from a glorious golden lampstand which stood directly opposite the table. Made in one piece of solid beaten gold it weighed about 43 kg. In Hebrew it is known as the 'menorah' and has developed into one of the most commonly used symbols of Judaism.

It was a work of extraordinary beauty and consisted of three main parts: the base, the shaft and the branches. Out of the base a vertical shaft arose and from either side of the shaft there sprang three branches curving outward and upward.

Each of the six branches and the centre shaft ended in a cup made in the form of an open almond flower. The opened petals of the flower held an oil lamp.

The branches and the central shaft were skilfully decorated with that same open-almond blossom motif with three on each branch and four on the centre shaft. The decoration was so exquisite and intricate that God insisted it should be made only by the most highly skilled craftsmen.

The seven oil lamps resting in the flower petals were like saucers and would probably have the rim pinched in at one

end. A flax or linen wick would be placed in the lamp and protrude from the neck at that point.

Twice every day, morning and evening, a priest attended to the wick and replenished the pure beaten olive oil of the sacred lamps (30:7). They were always kept burning (27:20; Lev. 24:2). All day and all night, whether anyone was present or not, these seven lamps constantly lit up the glory of the Holy Place.

These continually burning lights have a message for our lives. Human nature tends to work on the principle that we ought to shine when others are present to observe us. God's principle is that whether we are in the presence of others or not, we are always in his presence and the light of our lives should constantly be giving glory to him. At the close of the instructions God gave regarding the making of this piece he stated its purpose very simply as being 'so that they light the space in front of it' (25:37).

In a dark place it had to illuminate the scene seven times over and so long as the lampstand gave out its light there could be no darkness in the Holy Place. When the Apostle

John wrote of Jesus he referred to him as 'light' saying, 'The light shines in the darkness; but the darkness has not overpowered it' (John 1:5 marg.). That is the principle of the light in the tabernacle.

But John went further and announced the glorious news that in Christ, 'The true light that gives light to every man was coming into the world' (v. 9). He spoke of God made man in Jesus Christ and exclaimed, 'We have seen his glory' (v. 14).

When he came, Jesus identified himself, using that very symbol of light. He said, 'I am the light of the world. Whoever follows me will never walk in darkness, but will have the light of life' (John 8:12). Thus when we think of the lampstand constantly giving out light it reminds us that Christ has not only brought light, but is himself the light of life to us.

In the Old Testament God spoke of light representing his presence amongst his people. The benediction which we often use was composed by God to be spoken by his priests:

> The Lord bless you and keep you;
> The Lord make his face shine upon you
>   and be gracious to you.
>
> (Num. 6:22ff.).

His face had shined, his grace had come into the world and, as Jesus said, 'whoever lives by the truth comes into the light' (John 3:21).

When we think of the oil in the lamps we may also think of Zechariah's vision in which it was revealed to him that the pure olive oil feeding seven lamps is a picture of God's Spirit (Zec. 4:1–6). He is the one who comes into our lives and changes darkness to light. As Paul wrote to the Ephesian Christians, 'For you were once darkness, but now you are light in the Lord. Live as children of light ... be filled with the Spirit' (Eph. 5:8, 18).

The lamps shining from the lampstand lit up a scene where everything solid was either made from, or overlaid with gold. The remainder was beautifully woven material.

The seven lights showed the glory of the solid gold lampstand on which they were placed, and of the table opposite with its Presence bread, and also of one further item of furniture. This stood in a central position as close as possible to the veil dividing the Holy Place from the Most Holy Place. It was the Gold Altar of Incense.

This third piece of furniture in the room was a small altar on which incense was burned. Made from acacia wood overlaid with pure gold it stood higher than any other, the top being 2 cubits (1 metre) above the ground. Its top surface was a square area one cubit each way and it had around it a crown of gold. Small golden horns projected from the four corners in similar fashion to the altar in the courtyard. Lower down on each side there was a golden collar to hold a pole for carrying purposes.

This altar was used for burning incense, which twice every day was offered by the priest after he had tended the wick and oil of the sacred lamps. Its horns were also sprinkled with blood in connection with the sin offering regarding either a priest or the whole Israelite community.

The incense was a mixture of three rich and rare spices which cannot be identified today. These were blended with frankincense and beaten to a fine powder to which salt was added. It was totally forbidden for this formula to be used by any private individual. It had to be distinctive to the worship of God.

The incense was burnt on pieces of hot coal which the priest removed in a censer or firepan from the altar of burnt offering in the courtyard. A censer apparently consisted of a shallow bowl or pan, to which a handle was fixed. It could be used subsequently for removing the cold ashes from the altar or gathering up the burnt parts of wick from the lampstand.

Scattered on burning coals the incense produced a delightful fragrance in the Holy Place and clouds of smoke rose upward, wisping their way through the tabernacle curtains. As early as the time of Noah, when he had been rescued from the deluge and in gratitude to God built an altar and offered burnt offerings on it, we are told that the odour rising from the altar was pleasing to God (Gen. 8:21). The obedience of Noah in approaching God by way of shed blood was pleasing to God. His faith and obedience were pleasing to God. The fact that, in worship freely expressed, his first act should be a spontaneous offering was pleasing to God.

And within the tabernacle an offering which succeeded a sacrificial offering took place. It was the offering of the person whose sins had been forgiven by blood and who then went on to express the fragrance of love and worship. And this too was most pleasing to God.

The Gold Altar speaks to us of the worship of God's people who, in the Holy Place, are united in adoration of him. But you cannot have the incense of worship without first having the burnt altar of sacrifice. Praise can only be based on sacrifice. The coals which ignited the incense had first of all to be carried from the altar of sacrifice to the altar of incense. So the two altars were brought into association, and without the first there would be no fragrant incense ascending from the second.

Worship is only pleasing to God when it is offered by those who have been to the altar and, laying hold of the lamb of sacrifice, have had their sins forgiven. As Amelia Hall expressed it in her hymn:

> I have been at the altar and witnessed the Lamb
>   Burnt wholly to ashes for me;
> And watched its sweet savour ascending on high,
>   Accepted, O Father, by thee.

To those who *have* been there, there is another savour in the Holy Place. It is that of communion and prayer together with the adoration and worship of God. As Jesus himself said to the Samaritan woman, 'A time ... has now come when the true worshippers will worship the Father in spirit and truth, for they are the kind of worshippers the Father seeks' (John 4:23). These are the people who go into the Holy Place and burn fragrant incense on the Golden Altar.

But although a priest would burn these hallowed spices on the altar over 700 times in a year he knew that no priest other than the High Priest could go beyond that point, and even he would do so on only one single day (Lev. 16:2ff.; Num. 18:7; Heb. 9:7). The incense altar was placed as near as possible to the Most Holy Place but at all times there was a veil which shut off the one from the other.

It was of the same type and pattern as the cherubim-decorated curtains surrounding the Holy Place, but it was of a special order and called 'the curtain of the Testimony' or 'the veil' (26:31; Lev. 24:3). It was hung by gold hooks from four wooden pillars overlaid with gold.

The word 'veil' means that which covers or conceals, and this curtain concealed the holy room that lay beyond. It was a barrier to any man other than the High Priest

entering the presence of God, and on 364 days in a year it was a barrier even to him.

When the tabernacle was replaced by the temple it also had a curtain in the same place. In the temple this was of much greater size and thickness. According to an* account dating back to temple times the veil before the Most Holy Place was 40 cubits long and 20 cubits wide (18 metres × 9 metres). It was made out of 72 squares which were joined together and was the thickness of the palm of the hand.

When Jesus died a most remarkable thing happened. Matthew records it in these words; 'At that moment the curtain of the temple was torn in two from top to bottom' (27:51). This meant the path into the presence of God was uncovered and all are now invited to enter through the way Christ opened.

*Alfred Edersheim *The Life and Times of Jesus the Messiah* Part Two, p. 611 (Pickering & Inglis).

But while that curtain still hung in the tabernacle, it concealed the most sacred piece of furniture in the whole worship pattern. This was the Ark of the Covenant of the Lord or Ark of the Testimony. On the open ark rested the atonement cover traditionally known as the Mercy Seat. Although at first sight the ark might appear to be one item of furniture, it did in fact consist of two distinct pieces which were so closely combined that they formed a unity.

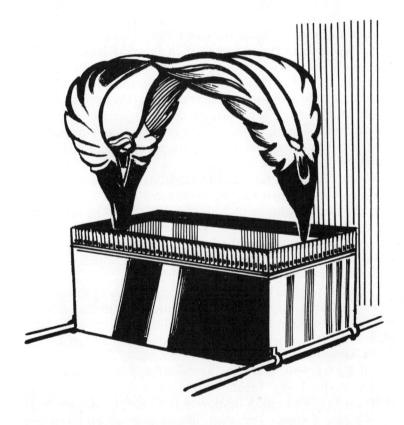

The ark was a rectangular wooden chest overlaid with pure gold, inside and out. Two-and-a-half cubits long by one-and-a-half cubits wide and high ($1\frac{1}{4}$ metres $\times \frac{3}{4}$ metres) it had a gold moulding or rim encircling the top. The ark rested on four gold rings which acted as feet through which the gold carrying poles were inserted and left permanently in position.

The Ark of the Testimony was the high point of Israel's worship. It is referred to 191 times in the Old Testament. Sometimes it is called the 'ark of the Covenant of the Lord'. In the songs of Israel it was known as the 'ark of your might' (Ps. 132:8). The most comprehensive name was the 'ark of the covenant of Yahweh'* (Num. 10:33) because it contained the two tablets of the Decalogue (the Ten Commandments) which were the basic documents relating to God's redemptive covenant with Israel. Historically God had made a remarkable covenant with Israel, but the people had broken it. In grace God renewed it and ordered that its enduring record should be deposited in this holy chest. The Book of the Covenant, which dealt at length with other aspects of law and procedure, was deposited alongside the ark. But the heart of God's divine and moral law was stored within the ark itself.

When God referred to the tablets of the law and gave these particular instructions to Moses, he said, 'Put in the ark the Testimony, which I will give you' (25:16). This shows that the tablets of the law were more than a schedule of commandments revealing sin in mankind. They were a 'testimony'. They testified to the salvation which God in a sovereign-ruler covenant relationship with his people provided for those who remained loyal to his covenant.

Two other items were also contained within the ark. One was a jar containing an omer ($2\frac{1}{4}$ litres) of manna (16:33; Heb. 9:4). It was a memorial of God's provision as he said, to be kept 'for the generations to come, so they can see the bread I gave you to eat in the desert' (16:32). It was also a token of the living bread which came down from heaven (John 6:51). The third item which would be added in the future was Aaron's rod that sprouted buds and blossoms and bore ripe almonds in a night, so authenticating his priesthood (Num. 17:8; Heb. 9:4).

*or, the LORD.

Now in itself the Ark of the Covenant was a golden chest open at the top. The atonement cover or Mercy Seat which God prescribed was a plate of solid gold the same size as the top of the Ark.

At each end of the Mercy Seat, and of one piece with it, were two hammered gold cherubim facing one another. Their outstretched wings overshadowed the gold plate and their faces constantly looked down upon it. They were symbols of the presence and holiness of Yahweh and as such they surrounded the sacred centre of the Most Holy Place.

After the covenant had been ratified by the people of Israel, one of the first things God told Moses on the mountain was that he would 'dwell among them' (25:8). Before Moses left Sinai God had gone on to say again, 'I will dwell among the Israelites and be their God. They will know that I am the LORD their God, who brought them out of Egypt so that I might dwell among them' (29:45, 46).

When God made his dwelling place among the thousands of Israel and said, 'There ... I will meet with you', he specifically stated, 'above the cover (mercy seat) between the two cherubim that are over the ark of the Testimony, I will meet with you' (25:22).

So the outstretched wings of the cherubim were to provide a throne for the God who is unseen, but nevertheless the God who is there. 'Hear us, O Shepherd of Israel ... you who sit enthroned between the cherubim,' is the cry of the psalmist (Psalm 80:1; cf. 1 Sam. 4:4).

God, who had spoken to Moses out of the midst of the cloud upon Sinai, had told his servant that he would come down to speak with him in the midst of his people. It was from the space above the atonement cover that he could do so and we read in the record that 'When Moses entered the Tent of Meeting to speak with the LORD, he heard the voice speaking to him from between the two cherubim above the atonement cover on the ark of the Testimony' (Num. 7:89).

The fleeing Jacob, father of the Israelite people, had on one occasion heard the voice of God in a place which he then named Bethel, the house of God. He woke in fear saying, 'How awesome is this place! Surely the LORD is in this place, and I was not aware of it' (Gen. 28:17, 16). But when God spoke to Moses 'from between the two cherubim above the atonement cover', it was because Moses had come to the place where God had said he would be found. How awesome was that place. God was in that place—and Moses knew it.

In the place where God spoke the cherubim bore witness to his absolute holiness. They also formed a unity with what bore witness to his surpassing mercy—the Mercy Seat. In the New Testament this Mercy Seat or atonement cover is spoken of twice. It is referred to in Hebrews 9:5 where we read that the 'cherubim of glory (were) overshadowing the mercy seat' (RSV).

The Greek word for Mercy Seat is *'hilasterion'*. It is only used in one other place in the New Testament where Paul says (literally) in Romans 3:25 that God presented Christ as a 'mercy seat'. This means that God's mercy has been extended to us in Christ Jesus. For that Mercy Seat did not derive its worth from the purity of its gold but from the fact that it was the place where the blood of sacrifice was sprinkled in the presence of Yahweh.

This is why Paul says that 'God put forward Christ as a Mercy Seat (literally) by his blood, to be received by faith' (see Rom. 3:25 RSV). It is, as the apostle John declared, 'the blood of Jesus, his Son, (that) purifies us from every sin' (1 John 1:7). Christ crucified can therefore be for every man or woman what the Mercy Seat was for Israel—the meeting place where God can justly forgive sin.

12 | THE DAY OF ATONEMENT

The one day each year when the High Priest drew aside the protecting curtain and entered the Most Holy Place was the most hallowed in Israel. It has been described as the 'Good Friday of the Old Testament', and took place on the tenth day of the seventh month, Tishri. By our calendar that would be around the end of September or early October. It was a day of fasting (Lev. 23:26ff.) in which no work could be done.

The atonement effected was for the priesthood, for the people, and for God's dwelling-place the sanctuary, which he said, 'is among them in the midst of their uncleanness' (Lev. 16:16).

The purpose of the Day of Atonement was to avert God's anger for the sins of the past year and seek his continuing presence in the one that lay ahead. It was the day on which the meaning of the sacrificial system reached its highest point. For in spite of all the daily, weekly, and monthly sacrifices that had been offered, there was still sin that was not fully atoned for, and on this special day forgiveness would be sought for it.

It was also the day which showed in its clearest form the work of the High Priest as mediator between God and man. On this day, as representative of the people, he had access to the presence of God and the people shared this access in him. Insofar as he was received and accepted in the Most Holy Place and returned alive to show them so, they knew that their covenant-keeping God had once more extended his mercy to them. But this could not happen without repentance and confession of sin, without sacrifice, and supremely without the shedding of blood (Lev. 16; Ex. 30:10; Lev. 23:26–32; 25:9; Num. 18; 29:7–11).

The day began with personal preparation by Aaron for the solemn part he would play in this visual demonstration of the way of approach to God. Everything he would carry out in the complex ceremonies had a meaning that could be understood in relation to man's need of forgiveness.

Aaron first of all discarded his priestly regalia. His official garments which were for dignity and honour would not be seen at this time. Aaron was himself a sinful man and so he clothed himself only in white linen which was a symbol of his personal repentance together with the rest of the nation. This day he would be approaching God as a sinner seeking pardon.

Dressed in a plain long linen coat and headdress, with linen sash for a belt, he went forward under the eyes of thousands of concerned Israelites and passed through the entrance gate of the courtyard, leading a young bull and a ram. He had gone like any other repentant sinner to seek the forgiveness of God for himself and his family of priests.

He led the young bull to the burnt altar of sacrifice and there placed his hands on its head, confessed his own sin and that of his family, then slaughtered it. The animal was a substitute for Aaron and its blood was shed so that atonement could be made for his sins. Aaron took the blood of his sacrifice and placed it in a bowl. He filled his censer with coals of fire from the bronze altar on which selected parts of that sacrifice were burned to ashes. Then he washed his feet and hands at the bronze basin and entered the outer room of the tabernacle. From this moment onward he was hidden from view.

Passing through the Holy Place he gathered up two handfuls of the consecrated incense that lay there and then stood face to face with the curtain of the tabernacle. It was an awesome moment when he drew it back and stepped forward to enter the presence of God. In faith he moved the curtain, but was careful to carry the blood with him, for without the blood of sacrifice he could not live in the presence of Yahweh whose glory shone in the Most Holy Place—the throne room of God.

His first task there was to sprinkle the incense on the coals in the censer he was carrying so that the holy room might be filled with a cloud that would overhang the atonement cover. And then he did the most solemn thing of all. He took some of the blood and with his finger sprinkled it on the atonement cover below that place which was hallowed with God's presence. His last act was to sprinkle blood seven times on the floor in front of the ark.

To the relief of the people, a few moments later the High Priest emerged from the tabernacle. Aaron stood at the door of the Tent of Meeting (Lev. 16:7) while two goats were led toward him. He then cast lots. As a result one goat was chosen as the goat for the Lord while the other became the 'goat of departure' or 'goat of removal'.

The first goat was sacrificed just as Aaron's own offering had been, but this time it was the sins of the people which were identified with it. As their High Priest he laid his hands on it and as their representative he killed it for them.

Once more Aaron made the reverent journey by way of the Holy Place, through the curtain and into the Most Holy Place where that cloud of incense hung. Once again in supplication and worship he sprinkled the blood of the sin offering on the atonement cover, then seven times in front of it.

Normally the man who offered a sacrifice for his sin was obliged to stand far off from God's presence. But on this day the representative of every sinful man and woman was allowed to enter the Most Holy Place and be given the assurance that their sin had been forgiven by God.

History records that during this time the people outside stood in great fear. If the High Priest delayed, they became terrified that their sacrifice had not been accepted and he had been killed in the presence of God. If this should happen they themselves would be left as a people without hope.

However, when Aaron, with joyful gratitude to God, retired from the Most Holy Place he drew aside the curtain and went back into the Holy Place towards the golden altar. This day he did not approach it to offer incense but with his finger, sprinkled some of the blood on its four horns.

When, with a burst of joy and relief, the people saw their representative emerge from the Holy Place, the first thing he did was to go to the altar of burnt offering and in the same

121

way sprinkle its four horns with the blood of the bull and the goat.

The second of the two goats was still standing there. It was the goat of departure or removal, often referred to as the scapegoat, that is to say, the escape-goat. This goat would live, but the command was that it should 'be sent away into the desert' (Lev. 16:21). It was destined to be a vivid picture of sin being removed and never seen again.

David praised God saying, 'As far as the east is from the west, so far has he removed our transgressions from us' (Ps. 103:12). And this goat represented the removal of iniquities as he bore them upon him to an isolated place in the wilderness, never to be seen again.

Aaron laid both his hands on the head of the goat and confessed over him 'all the wickedness and rebellion of the Israelites—all their sins' (Lev. 16:21). In an act of symbolic substitution he laid them, as it were, on the head of the goat which was then taken far into the depths of the desert by a selected man who would release him, once he had made sure it was not possible for the animal to return.

The great ceremony was drawing to a close but Aaron still had to go back into the Holy Place, bathe his whole body in water, then come out to the people wearing his splendid apparel.

He had one more offering to make. It was a burnt offering which, as distinct from all other sacrifices, was wholly consumed by fire on the altar. When Aaron offered one ram for himself and one for the people it was an act of praise and worship to God for providing a way of atonement.

If we retrace the steps of Aaron on that momentous day, knowing what we now do of the person and work of Jesus Christ, we will find just how much the tabernacle pattern speaks of him.

Leaving his tent Aaron first made his way to the one and only entrance to all that lay beyond. No man could enter any other way. As Christ himself testified, 'I am the way ... no-one comes to the Father except through me' (John 14:6).

The first item of tabernacle approach to God which Aaron encountered was the Altar of Burnt Offering. It was the place where the blood of substituted animals flowed for sin. But Scripture says, '*We* have now been justified by his blood' (Rom. 5:9). The bronze altar was the place where never-ending sacrifices were continually burned. But Scripture says, '*We* have been made holy through the sacrifice of the body of Jesus Christ once for all' (Heb. 10:10).

Moving toward the tabernacle proper the High Priest paused to wash his feet and hands in the water of the bronze basin. Similarly Christ was the one who, 'wrapped a towel round his waist ... poured water into a basin and

(washed) his disciples' feet' (John 13:4, 5).

Entering the outer room, the Holy Place, Aaron saw on his right hand the bread of the Presence laid on the gold table. 'Then Jesus declared, "I am the bread of life ... I am the living bread that came down from heaven. If a man eats of this bread, he will live for ever"' (John 6:48, 50, 51).

The room was lit by one golden lampstand with its seven branches and seven lamps. 'When Jesus spoke again to the people he said, "I am the light of the world. Whoever follows me will never walk in darkness, but will have the light of life"' (John 8:12).

Moving forward Aaron came to the Golden Altar of incense—the twice daily place of worship. 'The wise men said of Jesus, "We ... have come to worship him". And they bowed down and worshipped Jesus. Then they opened their treasures and presented him with gifts of gold and of incense and of myrrh' (Matt. 2:2–11).

After this the High Priest came face to face with the curtain. It stood there to bar man's way into the Most Holy Place. But says Scripture, 'We have confidence to enter the Most Holy Place by the blood of Jesus, by a new and living way opened for us through the curtain, that is, his body' (Heb. 10:19, 20). And, as he hung upon the cross, his body was torn, and 'At that moment the curtain of the temple was torn in two from top to bottom' (Matt. 27:51).

When Aaron entered the Most Holy Place he was in the presence of the living God. And the divine Presence is made known in Christ, who said of those who were cleansed by his blood, 'There am I with them' (Matt. 18:20).

When Aaron dipped his finger in the blood of sacrifice it was to sprinkle it on the atonement cover. This was the ultimate act. Yahweh had said he would dwell between the cherubim above the atonement cover and it was because blood had been sprinkled there that he was able to regard sin as having been atoned for.

But for today the word of God brings us good news in the Most Holy Place. All who have sinned and fallen short of the glory of God may be 'justified freely by his grace through the redemption that came by Jesus Christ. God

125

presented him as (a mercy seat) a sacrifice of atonement, through faith in his blood' (Rom. 3:24, 25).

How then can we sum up this revelation of Christ which is inherent in the tabernacle plan as unfolded by God, other than in the words of Paul who said, 'Christ is all, and is in all'? (Col. 3:11)

When the day of atonement drew to its close the high point of the priest's task to act as mediator between God and man had come and gone, but only for one more year. Then it would be repeated one year later and every year from then on. It might have continued endlessly had it not been that something uniquely wonderful happened. A High Priest entered the world, who himself became the sacrifice for sin.

He was not only the sacrifice that would *cover* man's sin, he was also the sacrifice who would *bear it away* in his own body by giving his life for the people, and shedding his blood on behalf of each repentant sinner. Here was something man had not thought possible; a High Priest who offered himself to God and was accepted as the full and final sacrifice for sin.

The Book of Hebrews relates this truth to the pattern of tabernacle worship and demonstrates the way in which God the Son became, in Jesus Christ, the supreme High Priest beyond whom there is no other.

It impresses on us that this High Priest is not one who does not understand all our human problems and temptations. On the contrary, he became one of us that he might truly represent us to God the Father, 'For', says the writer, 'we do not have a High Priest who is unable to sympathise with our weaknesses, but we have one who has been tempted in every way, just as we are—yet was without sin' (Heb. 4:15).

He goes on to explain that Christ did not come as a son of Aaron, but rather as a priest of the order of a man named Melchizedek. Now Melchizedek, who lived in the time of Abraham, combined the offices of both king and priest. He was king of Salem and at the same time priest of God Most High (Heb. 7:1). Christ's coming in this way had been prophesied long before in the inspired writings of David in Psalm 110:4:

> Yahweh has sworn
>   and will not change his mind:
> 'You are a priest for ever,
>   in the order of Melchizedek'.

The writer emphasises those words, 'You are a priest forever.' At last permanence has entered the priestly task. He declares, 'Because Jesus lives for ever, he has a permanent priesthood. Therefore he is able to save completely those who come to God through him, because he always lives to intercede for them. Such a High Priest meets our need ... Unlike the other High Priests he does not need to offer sacrifices day after day, first for his own sins, and then for the sins of the people. He sacrificed for their sins once for all when he offered himself (Heb. 7:24-27).

The author then recounts the pattern of worship and approach to God. He speaks of the tent, the Holy Place and the Most Holy Place. He refers to the Ark of the Covenant and the 'cherubim of the Glory overshadowing the place of atonement'. But concludes by pointing out that the High Priest had to enter the inner room every year and his always having to carry more blood simply showed the inability of that pattern to bring completed salvation.

Let the word of God speak (Hebrews Chapter 9):

> When Christ came as high priest ... he went through the greater and more perfect tabernacle that is not man-made (v. 11).

> He did not enter by means of the blood of goats and calves; but he entered the Most Holy Place once for all by his own blood, having obtained eternal redemption (v. 12).

> Christ is the mediator of a new covenant (v. 15).

> For Christ did not enter a man-made sanctuary that was only a copy of the true one; he entered heaven itself, now to appear for us in God's presence (v. 24).

> He has appeared once for all ... to do away with sin by the sacrifice of himself (v. 26).

> When this priest had offered for all time one sacrifice for sins, he sat down at the right hand of God (Heb. 10:12).

The sacrifices of the old covenant were superseded by the sacrifice of the Lamb of God. A new covenant, also requiring the shedding of blood, was brought into effect by God and, as sovereign-ruler, he offers to include each of us in its scope.

It is a covenant where there is one mediator between God and men, the man Christ Jesus (1 Tim. 2:5). It is a covenant in which the High Priest not only presents the sacrifice to God but by his substitutionary death and consequent resurrection is himself the sacrifice. He offers his own blood which not only covers but takes away sin, for the 'blood of Jesus ... purifies us from every sin' (1 John 1:7).

His sacrifice is complete. It is perfect in every way, and that is why we read that when he 'had offered for all time one sacrifice for sins, he sat down at the right hand of God' (Heb. 10:11). He was the only one who could.

> 'Therefore, brothers, since we have confidence to enter the Most Holy Place by the blood of Jesus, by a new and living way opened for us through the curtain, that is, his body, and since we have a great priest over the house of God, let us draw near to God with a sincere heart in full assurance of faith, having our hearts sprinkled to cleanse us from a guilty conscience and having our bodies washed with pure water. Let us hold unswervingly to the hope we profess, for he who promised is faithful' (Heb. 10:19–23).

God's tent is no longer pitched in the desert. The blood of animals has ceased to flow in that never-ending pattern of sacrifice. Aaron and his priesthood do not mediate between God and man. The presence of God is not to be found above the wings of the cherubim.

For through the sacrifice of Jesus Christ atonement has been finalised, and those who trust him are assured that 'he is able to save completely those who come to God through him, because he always lives to intercede for them' (Heb. 7:25).

He is personally present in their lives for, as Paul said, 'Christ lives in me. The life I live in the body, I live by faith in the Son of God, who loved me and gave himself for me' (Gal. 2:20).

In the throne room of my life God works out his high purpose. And if 'Christ lives in me' it means that my life can become—God's Tent.

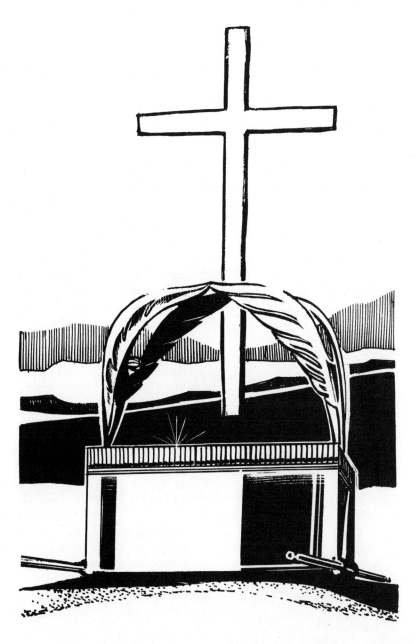

GLOSSARY

Different terms used in the undernoted translations.

Scripture Ref.	New International Version (NIV)	Revised Standard Version (RSV)	Authorised Version (KJV)
pp. 47ff.			
Ex. 26:1	The tabernacle	The tabernacle	The tabernacle
Ex. 27:21	The Tent of Meeting	The tent of meeting	The tabernacle of the congregation
Ex. 26:36	The tent	The tent	The tent
Num. 1:53	The tabernacle of the Testimony	The tabernacle of the testimony	The tabernacle of testimony
Num. 9:15	The tabernacle, the Tent of the Testimony	The tabernacle, the tent of the testimony	The tabernacle . . . the tent of the testimony
2 Chron. 1:3	God's Tent	The tent	The tabernacle
Acts 7:44	The tabernacle of Testimony	The tent of witness	The tabernacle of witness
pp. 106–111			
Ex. 26:33	The Holy Place	The holy place	The holy place
Ex. 35:19	The sanctuary	The holy place	The holy place
pp. 111–131			
Ex. 26:33	The Most Holy Place	The most holy	The most holy
Ex. 26:34	The Most Holy Place	The most holy place	The most holy place
Heb. 9:3	The Most Holy Place	The Holy of Holies	The Holiest of all
Ex. 26:33	The curtain	The veil	The vail

Scripture Ref.	New International Version (NIV)	Revised Standard Version (RSV)	Authorised Version (KJV)
pp. 83–87			
Ex. 30:28	The altar of burnt offering	The altar of burnt offering	The altar of burnt offering
Ex. 38:30	The bronze altar	The bronze altar	The brasen altar
pp. 89–94			
Ex. 30:18ff.	A (or the) bronze basin	A (or the) laver	A (or the) laver
Ex. 30:28	The basin	The laver	The laver
pp. 102–107			
Ex. 25:27	The table	The table	The table
Num. 4:7	The table of the Presence	The table of the bread of the Presence	The table of shewbread
pp. 107–109			
Ex. 25:31	A lampstand	A lampstand	A candlestick
Ex. 31:8	The pure gold lampstand	The pure lampstand	The pure candlestick
pp. 109–111			
Ex. 30:27	The altar of incense	The altar of incense	The altar of incense
Ex. 37:25	The altar of incense	The altar of incense	The incense altar
Ex. 39:38	The gold altar	The golden altar	The golden altar
Ex. 40:5	The gold altar	The golden altar	The altar of gold
Lev. 4:7	The altar of fragrant incense	The altar of fragrant incense	The altar of sweet incense

Scripture Ref.	New International Version (NIV)	Revised Standard Version (RSV)	Authorised Version (KJV)
pp. 114–116			
Ex. 25:17ff.	An (or the) atonement cover	A (or the) mercy seat	A (or the) mercy seat
Ex. 25:20	The cover	The mercy seat	The mercy seat
Heb. 9:5	The place of atonement	The mercy seat	The mercy seat
pp. 113–115			
Ex. 25:14	The chest	The ark	The ark
Ex. 25:22	The ark of the Testimony	The ark of the testimony	The ark of the testimony
Num. 10:33	The ark of the covenant of the LORD	The ark of the covenant of the LORD	The ark of the covenant of the LORD
Josh. 3:6	The ark of the covenant	The ark of the covenant	The ark of the covenant
1 Sam. 3:3	The ark of God	The ark of God	The ark of God
1 Sam. 4:6	The ark of the LORD	The ark of the LORD	The ark of the LORD
2 Chron. 6:41	The ark of your might	The ark of thy might	The ark of thy strength

DATE OF EXODUS

Alternatives:
Around 1440 BC   Early date
        1280 BC   Late date

LENGTH OF STAY IN SINAI:

Depart Egypt	*Month 1 Day 15*
Arrive Sinai	2 months later (Ex. 19:1)
Remain there during which time Moses on mountain, covenant made, broken etc.	
2 × 40 day periods + some days	3 months
Tabernacle completed	*Month 1 Day 1* (*of Year* 2)
	(Ex. 40:17)
Therefore tabernacle construction	$6\frac{1}{2}$ months (approximately)
Depart Sinai	*Month 2 Day 20* (*of Year* 2)
	(Numbers 10:11)
Thus making stay at Sinai	11 months and 5 days

BIBLIOGRAPHY

L. S. Chafer/Walvoord *Major Bible Themes* Zondervan.
Alan Cole *Exodus* Tyndale Press.
M. R. DeHaan *The Tabernacle* Zondervan.
Ed. by Lewis Drummond *What the Bible Says* Marshall, Morgan & Scott.
A. J. Flack *The Tent of his Splendour* G.L.S., Bombay.
Charles E. Fuller *The Tabernacle in the Wilderness* Revell.
R. K. Harrison *Old Testament Times* Eerdmans.
Roy L. Honeycutt *Exodus* Broadman Bible Commentary.
J. P. Hyatt *Exodus* Oliphants.
Glenn M. Jones *Big Ten Tabernacle Topics* Moody Press.
C. H. Mackintosh *Notes on the Pentateuch* Loizeaux.
F. B. Meyer *Exodus* Religious Tract Society.
J. A. Motyer *The tabernacle is the visible focus of the covenant.*
Martin Noth *Exodus* S.C.M. Press Ltd.
Stephen F. Olford *Camping with God* Loizeaux.
Charles E. Pfeiffer *Old Testament History* Baker.
Samuel Ridout *Lectures on the Tabernacle* Loizeaux.
R. J. Rushdoony *Institutes of Biblical Law* Craig Press.
Claus Schedl *History of the Old Testament* (5 *Vols.*) Alba House.
Samuel J. Schultz *The Old Testament Speaks* Harper & Row.
Samuel J. Schultz *Deuteronomy—The Gospel of Love* Moody Press.
A. B. Simpson *Christ in the Tabernacle* Christian Publications.
Henry W. Soltau *The Holy Vessels and Furniture of the Sanctuary* Kregel Publications.
Leon Wood *A Survey of Israel's History* Zondervan.

Bibliography

The International Bible Encyclopedia Eerdmans.
The Interpreter's Dictionary of the Bible Abingdon.
The New Bible Commentary Revised Inter-Varsity Press.
Lion Hand Book to the Bible Lion Publishing.
The New Bible Dictionary Inter-Varsity Fellowship.
New Westminster Dictionary of the Bible The Westminster Press.
The Wycliffe Bible Commentary Oliphants.
Wycliffe Bible Encyclopaedia (2 Volumes) Moody Press.
The Zondervan Pictorial Bible Dictionary Zondervan.
The Zondervan Pictorial Encyclopaedia of the Bible (5 Volumes), Zondervan.